D0031052

SAM ARNOLD'S

FRYING PANS WEST

This book is printed on mixed source FSC® paper.

Published by the Fur Trade Press™, LLC, Morrison, Colorado

Fur Trade Press™, LLC
P.O. Box 569
19192 Highway 8
Morrison, CO 80465
303-863-8803

Design by Barbara Scott Goodman

ISBN 978-1-4507-7963-0
Cooking/Regional Interest

Printed in China by Imago

10 9 8 7 6 5 4 3 2 1

Kinney, Holly Arnold
Arnold, Sam
Frying Pans West Cookbook and DVDs/
by Holly Arnold Kinney and Sam Arnold-1st ed.
ISBN 978-1-4507-7963-0
Cooking/Wine & Spirits, Regional Interest

Contents

Preface.. 6

Introduction.................................. 8

Meats Coming West....................... 10

Freshwater Fish & Seafood.............. 36

All Powerful Chile..........................46

A Trinity of Indian Foods.................. 58

Bread of the Frontier....................... 74

Frontier Desserts............................84

Frontier Drink.................................96

Mormon Foods...............................106

Christmas Specials.........................116

Where To Find It............................126

Index...128

If you love food and love history, as I do, this re-release of the *Frying Pans West* cookbook and 1960s PBS cooking show series is an absolute treasure. I'm sure many of us have had that experience of flipping through hundreds of television channels without finding anything worth watching. Put in one of these DVDs and what a contrast! Here is content that amuses, entertains, and educates at the same time.

Sam Arnold, known as the Ivy League Mountain Man, created this television series to share his own passion for cooking and for the history and culture of the American West. Bringing history to life, Sam prepared historic recipes and dispensed his well-researched knowledge one bite at a time. Filmed primarily in his home base of Denver, but also on location in such sites as Fort Laramie and the Pine Ridge Indian Reservation (Lakota/Oglala Sioux), this series explores the gustatory pleasures and cultural contours of diverse peoples and places in the American West. Sam had the careful eye of the historian and the true love of people of a master showman.

Sam Arnold, whom I first met through my own mentor, western historian and former president of Yale, Howard Lamar, was a delight. For many years, he brought his love of scholarship and his ability to make even an academic conference fun, to the annual meetings of the Western History Association. As a fellow Yalie, I am proud of his work and his spirit. Who else but a Yale man would build a full-scale adobe replica of Bent's Old Fort in Colorado? *Frying Pans West* is Sam Arnold's (Yale '47) magnum opus. Enjoy—but take it easy on the Taos Lightning—it packs a punch.

Dr. Jay Gitlin (Yale '71)
Associate Director,
Howard R. Lamar Center for the
Study of Frontiers and Borders,
Yale University

Preface

by Sam Arnold: 1968

The most frequent question asked of me is how I became interested in food and drink of the early West. Though I've always had an adventurous palate and enjoyed amateur cooking, the serious beginning point came in 1962. I'd bought some land in the foothills southwest of Denver and by sheerest chance, came across a picture of the old Bent's Fort, an historic fur trade fort of early Colorado. It looked like a castle made of adobe bricks. The idea of living in a fort fascinated me, and shortly I began construction of a full-sized replica to serve as my home. Within a year, it was completed, but, in order to pay the large mortgage, it was decided to turn a large part of the building into a restaurant.

Jumping into the restaurant business was an education. I had to learn how to cook for several hundred persons at the same time. My research into the history of Bent's Fort and the fur trade led me to reading journals and diaries from the 1830s. Sure enough, one of the most written-about facets of life in those times was meal time. Now, six years later, I've minutely examined some 1,600 books of the period. I still find new information and recipes. Many of the recipes are tried out on the Fort's adventurous customers.

Possibly the most outlandish recipe was "mouffle," or boiled moose nose. I was determined to try it. I asked my game purveyor in Montana to save me some moose noses, which arrived covered with thick hair and each measuring about three feet long. According to the French Fur Trapper recipe I'd found in Canada, the cook was instructed to put the nose on a stick and hold it over the fire until the hair burned off. I built a fire in

the courtyard of the Fort, and that evening customers walking by saw me roasting a long, ugly, hairy nose over it. The smell was hideous. Later I brushed the nose clean with a wire brush and soaked it overnight in salt water to remove any burnt hair flavor. The moose nose was then boiled with a bit of onion, bay leaf, peppercorn, and salt. It turned out to be dull and bland in flavor, with a consistency somewhat like a pickled pig's foot. I put it on the menu for $1.50 per portion, served cold and sliced with a piquant sauce. One evening, a disbelieving guest made a $100 wager with another guest that the "boiled moose nose" on the menu wasn't really moose nose. He lost.

Remember that cooking isn't a science. It's an art that comes from a familiarity with the characteristics of your ingredients combined with your own creative touch. Recipes are only like roadmaps...how you travel and where you end up depends on you. Good luck....

--Sam Arnold, 1968

Introduction

by Holly Arnold Kinney

My father, Sam Arnold, had a passion for the West and the food of the 19th century. In 1967, when he was 42 years old, he created an interesting and entertaining television cooking show called *Frying Pans West.* A few years earlier in 1963, he had created a full-scale adobe replica of Bent's Fort, a famous Colorado fur trading fort that had its heyday in the 1830s.

In Red Rocks Country, just outside of Denver, Dad turned his fort into a restaurant that served the foods of the mountain men, American Indians, and Mexican traders and trappers who had populated the West in the 1800s. Decades after it opened, The Fort restaurant continues to serve "New Foods of the Old West." It has been described as a modern-day Bent's Fort since it is still an international "trading center," attracting U.S. Presidents, world leaders, and tribal chairmen from various Indian tribes. Many of The Fort's customers are descendents of those who lived or traded at the original Bent's Fort. The Fort restaurant is known for truly authentic Colorado cuisine and sells more than 70,000 buffalo entrees a year! In this television series, you will see buffalo bone marrow cooked as it's prepared for today's customers in the same way it was in the 19th century.

I am now carrying the torch, as the sole proprietress of The Fort restaurant (www.thefort.com) . In 1999, my father and I created a non-profit organization in Colorado called the Tesoro Cultural Center (www.tesoroculturalcenter.org) to continue our mission of teaching Southwestern cultural history, including Bent's Fort history, to the public through school tours, lecture series, and two annual festivals: the Indian Market Powwow and the Spanish Colonial Market and 1830's Rendezvous. Both are events that celebrate life as it was lived in the Old West in the 1830s.

In 1967, Sam'l was working towards his master's degree at Denver University. He read diaries written by pioneers, visited museums and spent time with Indian tribes in his quest to learn about the foods of the American West. The *Frying Pans West* television series shares his adventures and research from that time, and also gives the viewer easy-to-make frontier-style recipes.

Thanks to Cal Reins and the film crew at KRMA Public Television in the 1960s. PBS offered the series to public stations across America and it aired for more than 15 years nationally. More than 100,000 of the accompanying cookbooks were sold during that time! Although *Frying Pans West* went off the air in 1983, many people continue to ask for the cookbook to this day.

My father passed away in 2006, but before he left us he knew I wanted to find the original master of the television series. I contacted Rocky Mountain PBS for help. Don Kinney of KRMA was already on the hunt for the shows and three years later we found the master in Washington, D.C., where it was in danger of being destroyed. We rescued it, digitized the film and now it is available as a DVD with this cookbook. Thank you Rocky Mountain PBS and especially Doug Price and Don Kinney for finding these treasured shows.

Also, a big thank you to my publishing "dream team": Mary Goodbody, my editor; Lester Goodman, my creative director; food historian/cookbook author and recipe tester, Beverly Cox, who tested these adventurous recipes; and Barbara Scott-Goodman, my book designer. Also thank you to my husband Jeremy Kinney who encouraged me to carry on The Fort because "It is in your blood…your destiny!" and to my executive assistant, Mary Pappas, who has planned many meetings and phone conferences, made sure the bills are paid, and is so thoughtful of others.

CHAPTER 1

Meats Coming West

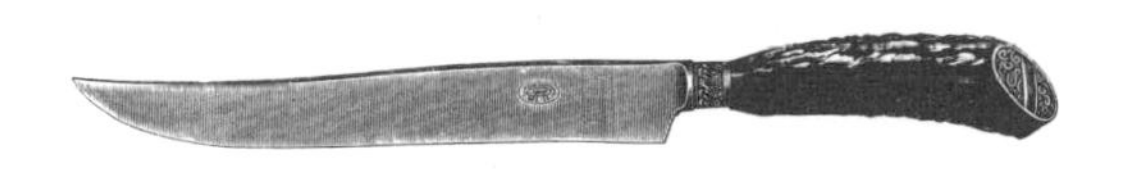

"Wagons HO!!"

The primary meat staple of the trappers, explorers, French voyageurs and wagon train immigrants seeking gold or land in the Great West, was salt pork. Why was it such a basic food? Because it was preserved with salt and could travel without spoiling. Plus, it tasted good and was easy to prepare. Another popular meat was buffalo, also known as the bison, which when these travelers first journeyed west roamed the plains by the millions. They learned from the Indians how delicious all parts of the buffalo were, including the sacred meat: buffalo tongue or buffalo bone marrow. The Indians taught the trappers and explorers how to dry the meat in strips and pound it with chokecherries and fat to create pemmican, another stable, portable, high-protein food that could be eaten on the trail. Most of the explorers, trappers, and others hunted deer, antelope, moose, and bear, too, as well as small game. There were several accounts of eating beaver tail, but the taste was described as "swampy." Like most of our ancestors who traveled West, I prefer salt pork and buffalo! *(Holly Arnold Kinney)*

Voyageurs' Pea Soup

French Canadian voyageurs, as the fur traders who paddled through the north country rivers and lakes were known, kept salt pork on hand, and often cooked it with dried split peas, another easy to carry and hard to spoil staple. They made a fire early in the morning and stoked the coals into a pile. A few slabs of sliced salt pork, a mess of split peas, and water went into a big iron pot. This was buried in the coals and left until the end of the day. Slowly simmered all day long, the dish was a famous voyageur mainstay — and a good easy one for anyone today.

We have instructions for cooking this the way the voyagers did, sitting between two mounds of hot coals in a dug-out pit in the ground. We also have instructions for making the soup on top of a stove.

serves 6 to 8

2 cups dried yellow or green split peas
1 medium onion, studded with 2 whole cloves
2 medium red potatoes, diced
6 ounces salt pork, in one piece
Kosher salt and freshly ground black pepper

1. Rinse the peas and put them in a 4- to 5-quart Dutch oven or large casserole with a tight-fitting lid with enough water to cover. Add the onion, potatoes, and salt pork.

2. Dig a hole in the earth that is deeper than the height of the Dutch oven and line the bottom of the hole with hot coals. Lower the Dutch oven into hole and cover it with more hot coals (you probably will need about 9 coals on top). This is called cooking "between two fires". Mound dirt around the pot and partially over the lid and coals. Let the soup cook throughout the day, replenishing the coals on top of the soup as needed. By evening you will find a hearty meal.

3. To cook on a stove, bring the soup to a boil over high heat, reduce the heat to very low, cover, and simmer for 2½ to 3 hours, stirring occasionally.

4. Remove the salt pork. Cut off and discard the fat. Dice the remaining lean meat and return it to the soup. Remove the onion and discard the cloves. Chop the onion and return it to the pot. Season to taste with salt and pepper and serve.

Salt Pork

IN THE MEAT DEPARTMENT OF SUPERMARKETS ACROSS the country are little packets of salt pork, all neatly wrapped and priced. They don't move rapidly and are bought only by the occasional cook who uses salt pork to flavor beans or soup. Yet, in the westward migration, salt pork was the mainstay of trappers, explorers and wagon train migrants. Lewis and Clark carried ample amounts of salt pork as a staple.

Why was salt pork such an essential food for these travelers? Preserved with salt, it could travel without spoiling; it flavored otherwise bland food; and it was easy to use.

Back in the days of the Oregon migration in the late 1840s, some enterprising authors, none of whom had traveled the trail themselves, wrote booklets advising the prospective pioneer what he would need to survive the long, arduous trip ahead. These booklets were bought by thousands of people eager for information, but they were often terribly misleading. For instance, they recommended stocking up on several hundred pounds of salt pork per person. By the time wagons, loaded with provisions, rolled up to Fort Laramie in eastern Wyoming, the horses were exhausted from pulling such weight. The settlers dumped their excess provisions; as a result, tons of salt pork were left behind in Wyoming.

Fried Salt Pork Gravy

Serve this with Hoppin' John for a good, easy Sunday supper, a fast lunch, or a good side dish for breakfast.

serves 6 to 8

8 ounces salt pork, cut into ½-inch-thick strips
1 tablespoon vegetable oil
3 tablespoons all-purpose flour
3 to 3½ cups milk
Kosher salt and freshly ground black pepper

1. Put the salt pork in a big pot and pour 2 kettles of boiling water over it to remove much of the salty taste. Discard the briny water. If you think of it, soak the salt pork overnight in water to cover, changing the water once or twice. If you do this, no need to start with boiling water. If you don't think of it, the boiling water works well. Pat the salt pork dry.

2. Heat the oil in a heavy skillet over medium-low heat and when hot, fry the pieces of salt pork until the fat is rendered and they begin to crisp. Remove the salt pork from the skillet and drain on paper towels. Pour off all but 3 tablespoons of the pan drippings. Add the flour to the pan and cook, stirring constantly, until the mixture is lightly browned and smooth.

3. Add the milk and stir to make a creamy gravy. Season to taste with salt and pepper and then return the salt pork to the pan.

Hoppin' John

In this recipe, I call for crisply cooked slab bacon with the Hoppin' John, but I also like the Fried Salt Pork Gravy on page 15, spooned over the black-eyed peas and rice. If you want to try it, leave out the bacon — although the bacon does give a fine flavor to the rice.

Hoppin' John is an old recipe that originated in South Carolina and is traditionally cooked on New Year's Day for good luck — as well as any other time during the year. It was carried west because its ingredients travel well.

serves 6 to 8

½ pound slab bacon
2 cups cooked canned or frozen black-eyed peas
1 cup long-grain white rice
½ cup shredded, sweetened coconut

1. In a large pot, cover the bacon with 4 cups of water and bring to a boil over high heat. When the water boils, reduce the heat to medium and simmer for about 30 minutes.
2. Add the black-eyed peas and rice to the pot, stir, and let the mixture return to a simmer. Cook at a simmer for about 20 minutes, or until the rice is cooked and the peas are soft. Lift out the slab of bacon and set aside.
3. Stir the coconut into the mixture and simmer over very low heat for 15 minutes longer.

4. Preheat the oven to 350°F.

5. Drain the peas and rice in a colander. Transfer the Hoppin' John to an oven-safe dish and bake for 6 to 8 minutes or until the rice is fluffy.

6. Slice the reserved bacon into pieces between ¼ and ⅓ inch. In a large skillet, fry the bacon over medium-high heat until nearly crisp. Drain on paper towels and then cut into 1-inch-long lengths.

7. Serve the Hoppin' John with the bacon scattered over the top.

★ PRAIRIE BUTTER

Another favorite of the Old West was bones cooked over a fire to soften the marrow. Trappers sitting around the fire took buffalo hip and leg bones, split them open and roasted them to get to the marrow. If they had good sourdough bread, they used it to sop up the marrow, which is how it got its name: "prairie butter."

Both Indians and trappers alike considered marrow an important food. It was eaten spread over bread and added to soups and stews. Even a type of dessert was made by cooking berries and marrow together. Eating marrow was popular in England at the same time, and to this day, some gourmet restaurants in London still serve marrow bones as a savory. Some antique stores in England and the United States sell special marrow scoops... a spoon with shaped with a long gouge to make it easy to dig out the marrow.

For your next party, ask the butcher to run some large beef thigh bones (femurs) through his electric saw lengthwise to expose the marrow. You can also ask him to cut them into 1½-thick discs. Roast the marrow bones in a 450°F oven for about 15 minutes. Watch the marrow as it cooks; you want it cooked but still gelatinous. Serve these hefty bones to your guests with fresh hot bread, explaining that they should spread the marrow over the bread as they would butter. It's delicious!

Jerky

HIKERS AND MOUNTAIN CLIMBERS HAVE DISCOVERED an early American food that provides energy and good eating... jerky.

Not only can you eat jerky in its natural state, but when camping, you can break it up, boil it in water and use it for meat stew. It absorbs the water and becomes plump and tasty. Salt the stew to taste, add prairie turnips or potatoes and regular white onions.

You can buy commercially made jerky in many taverns, but often it is simply a meat mash that has been extruded into strips and then baked. This is not real jerky and does not taste as good as the real thing.

Sun drying meat isn't new anywhere on the globe, but only in recent years has good jerky come onto our markets in quantity. It is light in weight and consequently good for the camper or hiker to carry. It's easy to make, too, but most people don't know how to cut a block of meat into strips suitable for drying.

Indians followed the natural contours and muscle layers of the beast when they butchered. They never cut across the grain or sawed through bones, as today's butchers do. Indians and the early mountain men often refused to eat meat that was cut across the grain.

To cut jerky, a very thin, flat razor sharp knife is needed. A hunting knife is too thick. A knife sharpened on one side only is the best to use. Cut the large chunk of meat into a rectangle or square (approximately three or four inches square). Next, cut into it from the thinnest side, cutting it almost in half, as if you were unrolling a jelly roll; maintain a ¼-inch thickness. (In a way, its like peeling an orange from the inside.) Cut this way, a chunk of meat will turn into a strip, sometimes three or four feet long.

Hang these strips, skewered on each end, high on poles so the dogs won't get them. I usually put a piece of cheese-cloth over the top to keep the flies away, but they rarely settle on the meat since it is cut so thin. In hot sun, it will dry in a couple of days. Take the meat inside at night so that it won't absorb moisture from the atmosphere and put it in a clean cloth or towel. In cloudy or rainy weather you can hang it indoors where there is good air circulation. I also put it in an open oven on the racks and set a fan in front of the stove to run all night. No heat, but lots of air. By morning it'll be jerked.

The Indians never added salt or pepper to meat. If you want to, you can, and peppered jerky is good eating. My favorite is to dredge the meat with an equal mix of Jamaican Pickapeppa sauce and Linghams Chili Sauce.

Washtunkala

While filming an episode of the Frying Pans West *television show at the Rosebud Indian Reservation in South Dakota, I discovered washtunkala, a stew the Sioux have made for generations. It is a delicious corn dish made with dried deer or buffalo meat and dried corn. The corn is left on the cob the year before and when the cook is ready to make the stew, the dried kernels are removed and soaked overnight in water to cover. The Indians put the kernels in jars but only filled them about two-thirds of the way — otherwise, the corn, which swells as it soaks, would not fit in the jar. Strangely, the rehydrated corn tastes almost like fresh corn again. The corn was next tossed into a big kettle filled with water and hung over a fire. To this, the Sioux added bite-sized pieces of dried meat, wild onions and prairie potatoes. Prairie potatoes taste somewhat like turnips and are often strung like garlic by the old Sioux people.*

serves 4 to 6

8 ounces beef, deer, or buffalo jerky, cut into bite-sized pieces

12 prairie potatoes, soaked overnight if dried, or 12 whole new potatoes, each 3 to 4 inches in diameter

One 15-ounce can corn kernels, undrained

½ onion, chopped

6 to 8 cups beef broth or water

1. Put the jerky, potatoes, corn, and onion in a Dutch oven or large pot. Add enough broth or water to cover by 1 inch.

2. Bring to a boil over high heat. Reduce the heat to low and simmer, covered, for 40 to 60 minutes or until the potatoes are tender and the jerky has softened. Do not add salt or pepper if you want the true Indian taste.

Indian Pemmican

It's fun to make real Indian pemmican for a camping trip. It travels well and is a good energy boost. The true Indian way is to mix chokecherries with fat. Chokecherries are blue-black wild cherries with large pits and little fruit (and not to be confused with their cousin, the chokeberry). They grow in clusters by waterways and can have a puckery flavor. When perfectly ripe, they are sweet and delicious. Indians gather chokecherries, dry them and make a mash of the cherries and their cracked pits. These little patties are left to dry in the sun. Before the chokecherries are used, they are broken up still further with a wooden mallet and then added to water for making was-nah (more on that on page 70). When making pemmican, use fresh chokecherries or sweet cherries, a close substitution. In the Indian way, the chokecherry pits were rarely removed but usually ground very fine. They add a certain grittiness to the Pemmican that some like. I don't!

makes 16 to 20 pemmican balls

Twelve 6- to 8-inch-long sticks beef, deer, or buffalo jerky, or ½ pound piece of dried meat (jerky)

½ pound white suet (fat from around kidneys)

1 cup fresh or frozen pitted cherries

1 to 3 teaspoons sugar

1. Preheat the oven to 350°F.

2. Put the jerky on a baking sheet and roast for 10 to 15 minutes, or until crisp like bacon.

3. Pound or put the jerky through a meat grinder with the suet (do not use a food processor).

4. Put cherries through the grinder with a little sugar.

5. Mix together the jerky, suet, and cherries and form into balls the size of chicken eggs. Transfer the balls to a plastic bag and refrigerate until ready to eat.

Note: You can melt a little additional beef suet in a pan and pour or pat the fat over the pemmican balls. This preserves them and keeps them moist.

Fort-Style Buffalo Tongue with Caper Sauce

Buffalo Tongue was perhaps the greatest delicacy of the 19th Century. A favorite of both President Ulysses S. Grant and Swedish singer Jenny Lind, bison tongue was served at all the finest restaurants including famed Delmonico's in New York. Buffalo Tongue is delicious. Smoother in texture than beef tongue, it makes a splendid dish when boiled.

serves 8 to 12 as an appetizer

1 buffalo tongue (about 2 pounds)

½ cup grated onion

1 teaspoon peppercorns

2 bay leaves

Dash of salt

Caper Sauce:

1 cup mayonnaise

2 tablespoons capers, drained

1 tablespoon prepared horseradish

Pinch of dried oregano

Pinch of freshly ground black pepper

1. In a large saucepot, cover the tongue with water. Add the onion, peppercorns, bay leaves, and salt and bring to a boil. Reduce the heat and simmer over very low heat for 2 hours.

2. Meanwhile, in a medium bowl, combine the mayonnaise, capers, horseradish, oregano, and pepper. Cover and refrigerate until ready to use.

3. Remove the tongue from the liquid and slice into thin pieces. Serve hot or cold with the caper sauce.

★ BUFFALO MEAT FOR TODAY'S TABLE

Buffalo meat is a little sweeter and richer tasting than beef and because the buffalo is not bred for meat production, fewer prime cuts are available. The price is also higher, in large part because demand outstrips supply. Buffalo has far less fat and is lower in cholesterol than beef. A mountain man of yore boasted that he could "eat two to three times as much buffalo as beef without being a glutton on that account." One man commented that "buffalo tastes like beef wished it tasted!"

From about 1880, when the buffalo herds were decimated, and until about 1960 when the herds began to come back, only a few bison were available for consumption. For years, the only buffalo sold were the few old animals culled from publicly owned herds. These would be turned over to various civic organizations for Buffalo Barbecues and very quickly buffalo meat got a bad name. Stringy, tough and strong, the old meat rarely made friends, especially when overcooked outdoors. When I began serving prime buffalo T-bones from two year old animals at The Fort restaurant, it was a miracle. When you once put a tooth to a tender buffalo T-bone or fillet, you find a whole new world.

Buffalo on the Prairie

VAST HERDS OF BUFFALO, ALSO CALLED BISON, ONCE covered the nation from coast to coast, with herds documented as far east as North Carolina. Estimates put the number of buffalo in America before 1800 at 70 million.

With the advent of the "white eyes" (European immigrants) hunting with heavy guns, mass destruction of the mighty bison became commonplace. By the 1860s, the only large herds remaining were in the remote northern plains states. So eager were people to kill buffalo, train excursions brought hunters to the West and the animals were shot from the trains. By 1883, buffalo were virtually extinct.

By the end of the nineteenth century, it was said that you could walk alongside the Northern Pacific Railroad tracks in North Dakota and never set foot on the ground for a distance of 100 miles. Instead, you walked on a carpet of dry buffalo bones. Sadly only the buffalo tongues and hides were prized by the white hunters and so bones were left behind.

By 1910, there were only 256 buffalo on the earth. Through massive conservation efforts, the buffalo were saved so that in the 1960s, more than 60,000 were living in the United States. Today, public and private herds total more than half a million animals. Most exist in commercial herds, including a large number in Yellowstone National Park.

Beefsteak and Oysters

A few years ago, I was rummaging through my family's attic looking for old books and turned up The American Cookbook, *dated 1885. Among the many interesting recipes was one for Beefsteak and Oysters, credited as a specialty of the famed Palace Hotel in early-day San Francisco. The Palace was dubbed the Waldorf of the Pacific and played host to many dignitaries and well known people, including King Kalakaua, the last king of Hawaii, and President Ulysses S. Grant.*

This is a superb dish, which may well have been developed by a Chinese cook at the Palace. The Chinese were known for liking the mix of flavors produced by beef and oysters. The small bay oysters found in the Pacific along the West Coast are excellent and should be used here whenever possible.

serves 1 to 2

2 tablespoons unsalted butter
½ cup shucked fresh oysters
1½ tablespoons all-purpose flour
¾ cup beef broth
Juice of ½ lime
1 teaspoon Worcestershire sauce, optional
Kosher salt and freshly ground black pepper
Pinch of garlic salt
One 8- to 12-ounce beef steak of your choice
1 tablespoon chopped red pimiento
1 tablespoon chopped flat-leaf parsley

1. In a saucepan, melt the butter over medium heat and cook the oysters until their edges curl. Remove the oysters with a slotted spoon and reserve.

2. Add the flour to the pan, stirring carefully to prevent lumps, and cook the roux for 2 to 3 minutes, until nutty brown. Add the broth and stir to make a medium-thick gravy. Stir in the lime juice and Worcestershire sauce, if using, and season to taste with salt, pepper and garlic salt. Return the oysters to the pan and stir gently. Cover to keep warm. If necessary, reheat gently.

3. Preheat the grill to medium-high or let the coals cook down until the heat is medium-high. Grill the steak to desired doneness. Remove from the grill and let the steak rest for about 5 minutes.

4. If serving 2, slice the steak and divide it between 2 plates. Otherwise, put the steak on a plate. Pour the oyster sauce over the steak and garnish with chopped pimento and parsley.

Music at Fort Laramie

PERHAPS THE GREATEST FORT OF THE OLD WEST, FORT Laramie was established in 1834 in eastern Wyoming, close to the Nebraska border. It was one of the most important stopping points on the Oregon Trail and during the height the mass westward migration in 1849, as many as 6,000 people a day stopped at the fort en route to California and the Northwest. Famed western painter, Alfred Jacob Miller, sketched the original fur trading fort, which later was replaced by a government military complex.

Today, Fort Laramie is one of the most interesting of our National Park Service sites. Buildings have been restored and furnished as they originally were. In 1963, a total restoration was completed by the National Park Service and as a special privilege, my wife and I were allowed to throw our sleeping bags down in an unfinished upstairs room at the old fort and spend the night.

The building creaked and emitted strange sounds, which frightened my wife. I poo-poo'd them and soon she fell asleep. As I lay there, still wide awake, I heard the distant sound of a band playing dance music, sounding as though it was drifting across a lake from a distant bandstand. The music continued for some time and then faded away. This was more than curious. Fort Laramie is in a remote area where no bands play, and certainly not at 3:00 in the morning!

Fort Laramie Chicken Salad

Elizabeth Burt was married to the colonel who was second in command at Fort Laramie when it was a busy location. She wrote a cookbook, now in our library at The Fort, and the family generously made the famous Fort Laramie Chicken Salad available to us for the television show.

The salad tends to be drier and more interesting than those found in delis and other take-out restaurants. Since, in the Old West, celery was only seasonally available, heads of cabbage were relied upon to add crisp crunch to winter salads. Cabbage kept very well in root cellars, and for this reason, Mrs. Burt included the suggestion of substituting cabbage for celery and advised mixing it with a teaspoon of extract of celery. Also, in the old days, the chicken was "boiled," although most likely it actually was poached.

serves 6 to 8

¾ cup mayonnaise
1 tablespoon fresh lemon juice
1 tablespoon cider vinegar
1½ teaspoons dry mustard
Kosher salt and freshly ground white pepper
1 chicken, poached
3 cups chopped celery (6 ribs of celery)
1 head leaf lettuce
3 large eggs, hard-boiled, sliced
1 cup pitted ripe olives
2 tablespoon capers
1 tablespoon chopped flat-leaf parsley

1. In a small mixing bowl, whisk together the mayonnaise, lemon juice, vinegar, and mustard. Season to taste with salt and pepper.
2. Remove and discard the skin from the chicken. Cut the meat from the bones and chop it coarsely. Transfer the chicken to a bowl and add the celery and half of the mayonnaise dressing.
3. Cover the bottom of a serving platter with the large lettuce leaves. Arrange the smaller green leaves around the border. Spoon the chicken salad on the lettuce and pour the remainder of the dressing over it. Garnish with sliced hard boiled eggs, olives, capers, and parsley.

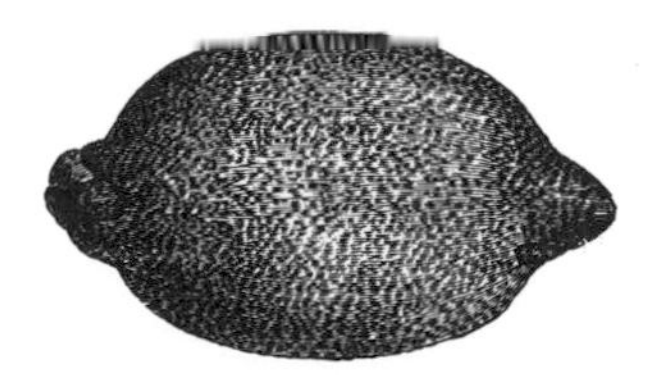

Swiss Enchilada

In Mexico, dishes are called "Swiss" simply because they include dairy products. Typical Mexican Swiss enchiladas are corn tortillas rolled around chopped chicken and onions, topped with red chile sauce and capped with sour cream. As tasty as these are, they can be varied by mixing chopped green chiles into warm sour cream mixed with grated Monterey Jack cheese. A dash of salt and Worcestershire sauce turns the creamy mixture into a splendid sauce.

For traditional New Mexico-style enchiladas, lay the tortillas flat in a shallow pan and sandwich layers of chicken meat and chopped onions between them, three tortillas high. Flood the top with the sour cream sauce and then put the pan under a hot broiler for only a moment or two to brown the top.
If you can obtain them, use blue Indian corn tortillas for a more primitive corn flavor. These are available throughout the Southwest and increasingly so in other markets across the country.

serves 6 to 8

2 tablespoons unsalted butter
18 corn tortillas
4 cups shredded cooked chicken
1 onion, thinly sliced
1 cup mild green chiles (poblano or canned), chopped
4 cups (16 ounces) shredded Monterey Jack and Colby cheese
2 cups (1 pint) heavy cream
4 tablespoons unsalted butter
1 teaspoon dried Mexican oregano leaves or other oregano
½ to ¾ teaspoon garlic salt
1 cup sour cream
1 cup pitted ripe olives
Strips of red pimiento

1. Preheat the oven to 350°F.

2. Butter a 9- by 13-inch baking dish and overlap 6 corn tortillas to cover the casserole bottom and reach half-way up the sides. Scatter half of the chicken over the tortillas. Scatter half of the onion over the chicken followed by half of the chiles and a third of the shredded cheese.

3. In a saucepot, heat the cream, butter, oregano, and garlic salt over medium-low heat until warm. Remove from the heat and stir in the sour cream. Pour a third of this over the food in the baking dish.

4. Layer 6 more tortillas over the top of the casserole. Layer with the remaining chicken, onions, chiles and a third of the sauce and cheese. Layer the remaining tortillas over the cheese. Pour the remaining sauce over the casserole and scatter the remaining cheese over all.

5. Bake, loosely covered with aluminum foil, until heated throughout, 50 to 60 minutes. Remove the foil and continue to bake, uncovered, for 10 to 15 minutes to crisp the top. The consistency should be damp with the melted cheese and tortillas, but not sloppy. Serve garnished with black olives and pimiento strips.

When we have large banquets at The Fort with up to 700 guests, it is necessary to make giant casseroles, each large enough to serve 40 or 50 people. Our Swiss Enchilada was created for this reason, but as all the ingredients have been used together for many centuries in Mexico, it could be everyday frontier fare of the most delicious order. It is a spectacularly good dish.

Rocky Mountain Oysters

We've had more fun with Rocky Mountain oysters than with any other single food. One guest at The Fort, who came from back East, badgered a server, demanding to know where Rocky Mountain oysters were from. After several requests, she blurted out; "They're bulls' balls!" And it was the truth....

In Colorado, Rocky Mountain oysters are calf testicles, removed when the steer are castrated. In sheep circles, you'll find "sheep fries," also very popular and sometimes served as mountain oysters in Texas. The testicles from tom turkeys are highly prized, as well, and in my estimation are the tastiest of them all. They are known in the trade as "turkey surprises," perhaps a reference to the turkey's mystified expression after the operation. (Actually, they're removed when the bird is processed.)

At castration time on the range, which is in the spring, the fries may be impaled on sticks and toasted over an open fire until cooked. This is reputed to be the best way to eat "mountain oysters."

serves 4 to 6 as an appetizer

2 pounds frozen Rocky Mountain Oysters (ask for veal, lamb, turkey)

1 cup all-purpose flour

Kosher salt and freshly ground black pepper

1 large egg, beaten

2 cups soda cracker crumbs or panko

2 cups cooking oil

Western Seasoning Salt:

1/4 cup garlic salt

1/4 cup ground black pepper

1/4 cup lemon crystals (citric acid crystals or sour salt, ground fine)

1. Dip the frozen balls into warm water to loosen the tough outer skins, which must be removed from the gland. If there is other flesh still attached, cut it away. Cut around the ball of meat with a sharp knife, cutting through the skin only, as you might cut an orange in order to peel it. Work your fingers under the cut and pull off the outer skin. It requires a little work to loosen the gland from the outer skin. Then, before it thaws further, slice each ball of meat into ½-inch-thick slices.
2. Put the flour in a shallow bowl and season with salt and pepper. Put the beaten egg in another shallow bowl, and the cracker crumbs in a third. Coat the meat in the flour and then dip them in the eggs, letting any excess drip off. Finally, coat the meat in the cracker crumbs.
3. In a deep, heavy pot or deep-fat fryier, heat the oil to 375°F.
4. Fry the "oysters" for about 3 minutes, until the crumb crusts are browned and crisp and they bob to the surface. Do not overcook as it will make them tough. You may want to do this in batches.
5. In a medium bowl, stir together the garlic salt, pepper, and lemon crystals.
6. Let the "oysters" drain on paper towels and sprinkle with my Western Seasoning Salt. Serve still hot, with toothpicks and a piquant chile sauce for dipping.

Note: You may also simply dredge them with seasoned flour and fry the "oysters" in oil. Or, if you prefer to charbroil them, dip them in oil and lay them across a screen over the fire, so that they will not drop through. Turn them once and do not overcook.

CHAPTER 2

FRESHWATER FISH & SEAFOOD

FISH WAS OFTEN A WELCOME CHANGE FOR THE mountain men and explorers who traveled the West. Buffalo and deer meat (the latter only called venison by Eastern "greenhorns") could become tiresome after a while, and a good fish dinner was a pleasant change.

The western streams and lakes provided trout, whitefish, catfish, sturgeon and other species that usually were either pan fried or broiled on sticks over campfires. Smoke-cooking was common, too. This was, and is, done by building a covered "box" of branches and leaves over a smoldering fire. Aspen wood, hickory, or apple provide a fine smoky flavor. The fish is impaled with a green branch lengthwise, from the tail through the body to the mouth, and kept away from direct heat as it cooks. Nothing is better eating!

Minted Trout

Mary Schlosser, a Taos Indian, gave me this recipe for Minted Trout, a favorite from her family who lived in the Taos pueblo in New Mexico.

Serves 4

1 large bunch fresh mint, wild or garden variety, thick stems discarded

½ cup olive or cooking oil

½ teaspoon kosher salt

Four 1- to ½-pound fresh trout (4 to 6 pounds total)

8 strips bacon

1. Reserve 12 of the largest mint leaves. In a small bowl, mix the rest of the mint with the olive oil and salt. Using the back of a spoon, mash the mint leaves so that they mix with the oil to release the mint's flavor and essence.

2. Fill the cavity of each trout with the oily mint leaves. Arrange 3 of the reserved mint leaves on each trout and bind them to the fish with 2 strips of bacon. Secure the bacon with a round toothpick.

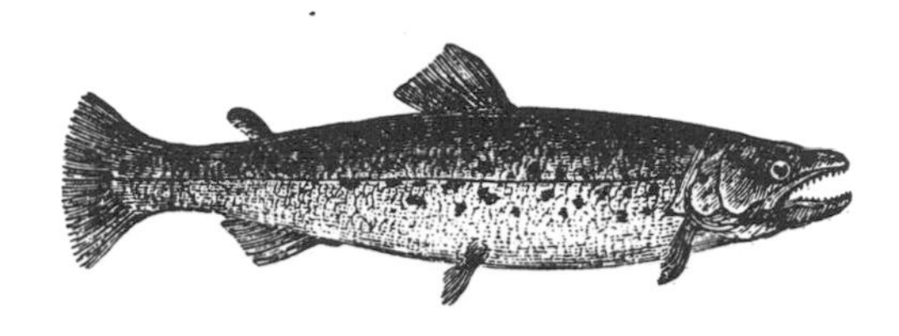

3. Prepare a charcoal or gas grill so that the heat is medium-high, or heat the broiler. Cook the fish until the bacon browns and crisps, 5 to 7 minutes per side. The bacon will baste the trout with its oils and flavor, and the mint will release its herbal taste, too.

4. To serve, remove all the mint leaves from the trout. The fish will not taste sweet, but will have a strange mystical herb flavor that's mighty fine eating.

Hangtown Fry

Hangtown Fry is a famous oyster recipe from California. According to legend, a miner who in 1849 was diggin' for gold in a remote area called Shirttail Bend, found his way to the town of Hangtown (today called Placerville). The Cary House Hotel was the only eating emporium in the area, and the miner demanded the most expensive meal they had. Eggs and oysters were the highest-priced items available And so the cook whipped up this dish for him. In those days, eggs cost more than a dollar each, and the price of oysters was even more astronomical.

serves 4

12 small, fresh, Pacific oysters,
shucked and liquid reserved
(use another kind of oyster if you can't find Pacific oysters)

½ cup all-purpose flour

Kosher salt and freshly ground black pepper

9 large eggs

1 cup soda cracker crumbs

½ cup (1 stick) unsalted butter

½ cup chopped red bell pepper

½ cup chopped green bell pepper

1. Gently dry the oysters on paper towels.

2. In a shallow bowl, mix the flour with the salt and pepper. In another bowl, lightly beat 1 egg. Spread the cracker crumbs in another shallow bowl. Dip the oysters, 1 or 2 at a time, in the flour to coat. Dip in the egg and let the excess drip off. Finally, coat the oysters with the cracker crumbs.

3. In a 10-inch non-stick skillet, heat the butter over medium heat and when melted, fry the oysters until the crumbs are browned, about 1 minute. Take the pan off the heat and leave the oysters in the pan.

4. In a mixing bowl, beat the remaining 8 eggs, as you would for scrambled eggs. Return the skillet to the heat, pour the eggs into the pan and cook over medium-low heat until firm, 2 to 3 minutes.

5. Sprinkle the chopped bell peppers over the eggs once they are cooked but still warm and soft. Serve immediately, sliding or lifting the eggs from the pan. (Do not fold like an omelet.)

Pickled Oysters

A favorite dish for many 19th Century people, including President Ulysses S. Grant, was Pickled Oysters. The president reportedly liked them better than almost any other food.

serves 6 to 8 as an appetizer

24 large oysters, shucked and liquid preserved
1 cup apple cider vinegar
1½ teaspoons kosher salt
½ teaspoon peppercorns, crushed
½ teaspoon allspice, crushed
1 stick cinnamon, 2 to 4 inches long
1 small hot red chile, fresh or dried, seeded and left whole

1. Put the oysters and their liquid in a pot and add enough water to cover by about 1 inch and cook over medium heat until the water barely begins to boil. Add a little salt. Skim off any foam that rises to the surface. Remove the oysters and set aside on a plate to cool.
2. Add the vinegar to the liquid in the pot, along with the salt, pepper, allspice, cinnamon, and hot chile. Heat to a boil over medium-high heat to release the flavor of the spices.
3. Transfer the oysters to sterile jars and pour the hot pickling juice over them. Let them cool and then cover tightly and refrigerate. The oysters are ready to eat in 2 days and are delicious. They will keep for about 1 week.

Oysters in the American West

OYSTERS WERE FREQUENTLY EATEN IN THE AMERICAN West. They were brought west by wagon and were iced at every stop with ice from the local ice house. To insure they stayed fat and healthy, those in charge of them poured salt water and cornmeal into the barrels holding them. This kept them hydrated and fed and they were able to travel for miles, as long as the water and cornmeal was replenished every so often. President Abraham Lincoln was famous in Illinois for his oyster roasts, given for voters in election season, and while this meant the oysters got as far west as Illinois, they also turned up on New Mexico and Colorado.

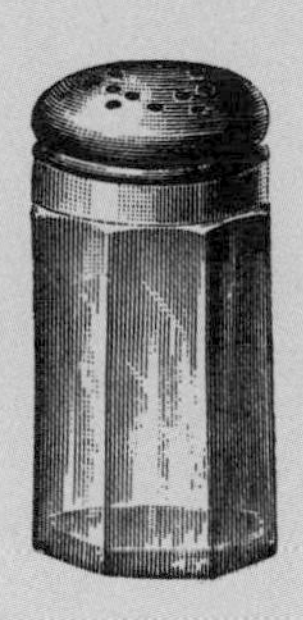

Planked Salmon with Huckleberry-Honey Glaze

The huckleberry is a wild cousin of the blueberry, in season in the late spring and summer months. This coincides with salmon runs in the rivers of the Pacific Northwest. The two foods are often served together, as they are here. Cooking the salmon fillets on alder or cedar planks gives them a mildly smoky flavor. The planks are sold in specialty markets, fish stores and some supermarkets, but if you can't find them, grill the salmon skin sides down on sheets of aluminum foil, basting the fillets with the glaze. You could also broil them.

serves 4 to 6

2 alder or cedar wood cooking planks

4 to 6 salmon fillets, skin on (about 6 ounces each)

Salt (preferably sea salt) and freshly ground pepper

6 tablespoons unsalted butter

3 tablespoons honey

2 tablespoons Dijon mustard

¾ cup fresh or frozen huckleberries or blueberries

2 tablespoons olive oil

1 lemon, cut into wedges

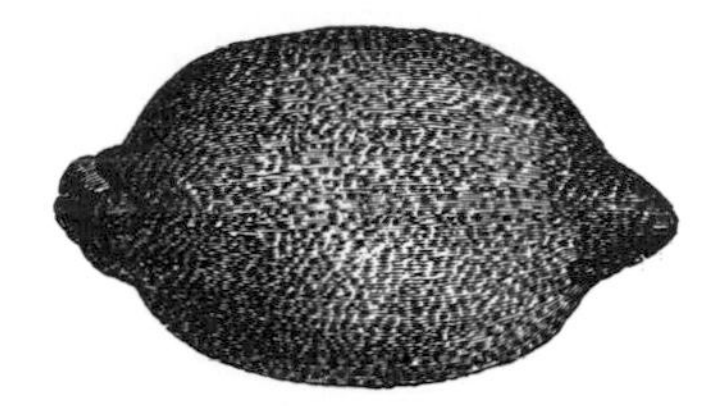

1. Soak the planks in water to cover for at least 1 hour before cooking the fish.

2. Put the soaked planks on the middle rack and preheat the oven to 400° F.

3. Rinse the salmon under cold running water and pat dry with paper towels.

4. In a small saucepan, heat the butter, honey, and mustard, stirring over low heat until the butter melts. Add the huckleberries and stir gently over low heat for 1 to 2 minutes, pressing and crushing some of the berries with the back of the spoon to make a slightly thickened sauce.

5. Brush the skin sides of the fillets lightly with oil and arrange them, skin sides down, on the hot planks. Sprinkle the fillets with salt and pepper and brush them with the huckleberry sauce.

6. Roast the salmon on the planks for 10 to 15 minutes or until cooked to your desired degree of doneness.

7. Heat any of the remaining huckleberry sauce and spoon it over the salmon with a squeeze of fresh lemon juice.

CHAPTER 3

All Powerful Chile

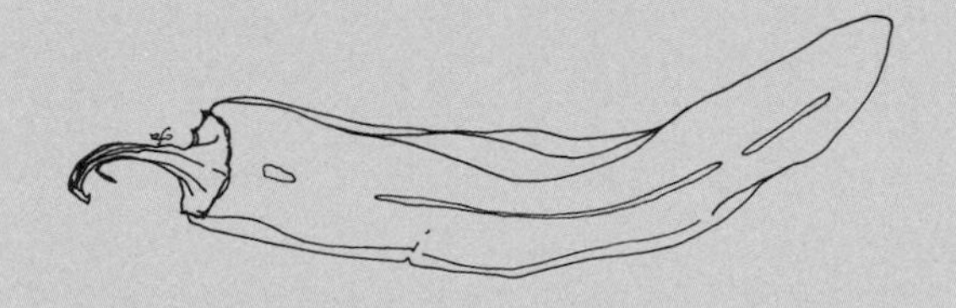

DO I SPELL IT "CHILE, OR CHILI?:

The ancient Capsicum genus, or chile, is one of the oldest cultivated crops in the Americas, having been domesticated for more than 7,000 years. As early as 1600, it was being cultivated by the Spanish colonists who settled in the Rio Grande valley in Northern New Mexico.

The word "chil" is derived from the Nahuatl (Aztec) dialect and refers to plants known as Capsicum. The correct spelling is chile, with the "e" at the end, and is the authentic Hispanic spelling of the word. English linguists have changed the spelling to "chili," which is best known as the state dish of Texas rather than the pepper.

The ancient and current day residents of New Mexico and Colorado dry chiles as a way to preserve them for use all year long. If you buy a ristra — a large bunch of chiles — be sure it isn't shellacked unless you plan to use it only as an ornament. The beautiful chile ristras come in many shapes and sizes, but the most common are made from red Anaheim peppers put together in strands that measure from three to six feet long. In New Mexico and Colorado, they are sold fresh at roadside vegetable stands in the fall, after the chile harvest. If you buy yours from one of these, be sure to hang it outside for two to three weeks on a covered porch so that it can dry. Otherwise the peppers could mold.

Basic Red Chile Puree

It's easy to make a fine chile puree. Often families in New Mexico toast dried red chiles in the oven for a little while before making the puree, which gives them a slightly different flavor. My preference is not to toast them. Try it both ways and decide for yourself. I like to scrape or rinse out the seeds, which tend to be very hot. This trick tames the heat. Try the puree over fried or scrambled eggs in the morning.

makes about 1 cup

6 to 8 dried, mild-to-medium-hot red New Mexican or guajillo chiles

½ teaspoon kosher salt

½ teaspoon dried Mexican oregano leaves

1 clove garlic, peeled and coarsely chopped

1. Stem the chiles and rinse out the seeds. Put the pods and ¾ cup of warm water in the container of a blender. Add the salt, oregano, and garlic. Blend into a smooth puree.

2. Press the puree through a coarse strainer. You now will have the finest chile sauce.

★ MEXICAN OREGANO AND OTHER OREGANO

While Mexican oregano is not the same plant as the oregano from the Mediterranean, it has a similar flavor. Like its distant cousin, Mexican oregano grows on rocky slopes and hillsides, but is more savory and stronger tasting. It is well suited for spicy dishes and is used extensively in Mexico and throughout Central America in salsas, chilies, and similar dishes. If you cannot find it, substitute the "other oregano."

Carne Asada

This cooked meat dish is a good use for Basic Red Chile Puree. If you use wooden skewers, soak them in water for about one hour.

serves 4 to 6

2 to 2½ pounds beef, 3- to 4-inches thick, or four 8-ounce sirloin flap or skirt steaks

¼ cup Basic Red Chile Puree, page 48

¼ cup cooking oil

1 clove garlic, minced

½ teaspoon kosher salt

½ teaspoon dried Mexican oregano leaves

1. Cut the meat into cubes about four of five inches square. With a sharp, thin-bladed knife, cut it into a long strip about ½-inch-thick, using the technique described for making jerky on page 18. This is an interesting technique, but it requires practice. You could ask for help from the butcher at a Latin American meat market. An easier method is to use sirloin flap or skirt steak and pound it until it's about ½-inch-thick. With either technique, cut the thin pieces of meat lengthwise into 3-inch-wide strips. Impale the strips of steak on wooden or metal skewers.

2. In a small bowl, stir together the puree, oil, garlic, salt, and oregano. Swab the meat with the sauce while grilling or broiling. It flavors the meat with a deliciously bite-y taste.

3. Prepare a gas or charcoal grill so that it is medium hot, or heat the broiler. Grill or broil the meat for 1 to 3 minutes per side, depending on how you like your meat.

What I Know About Chiles

THE FIRST EUROPEANS ARRIVING IN NEW MEXICO were greeted with a shocking new culinary experience: the chile pepper. Although black pepper and red cayenne pepper were well known in Europe, both the fresh and dried chiles found in the Southwest were totally new. Then, as now, while the initial meeting was hot and unpleasant, after repeated exposure to the chile, most people become virtual addicts and these immigrants were no exception.

I am one such addict. Most meals without chile in some form or another seem as bland to me as those without salt. After eating a bowl of good hot red or green chile, you have an unusual sense of contentment and tranquility.

Chiles grow in many variations of size and type, from tiny chile piquin and miniature raisin chiles to some that are two or three inches long, such as the popular green jalapeno. Some, like the chile poblano, are seven or eight inches long and may be green or red. The only difference between the red and green chile is that when allowed to fully ripen, the green will turn red. Every chile has its own flavor and its own degree of heat. They may be used fresh, dried, canned, or frozen.

A chile's heat comes from an oily substance called "capsaicin," generated in little globules on the inside ribs of the chile. If these are undisturbed, even the hottest chile will taste like a sweet pepper, but rarely does this happen. Bumping, picking, packing or just the act of pulling the chile off the plant ruptures the globules so that the burning hot oil spreads inside the pod. Each chile, even those growing on the same plant, has slightly different amounts of capsaicin, so there is no way to count on a uniform heat index from chiles. Generally, the California Anaheim chile has been bred to be least hot of the big green chiles commercially marketed. My friends from New Mexico never remove all the seeds, for they believe they provide an important vitality and flavor.

Stewed Hen in Red Chile

My father, Sam'l, turned up some fascinating material when he researched chiles and the food served in the Old West. For instance, he studied Susan Shelby Magoffin's diary. As a young bride, Susan was one of the first Anglo women to travel the Santa Fe Trail and when she and her husband Samuel spent two days in El Paso del Norte, she wrote this about the food — it's very likely she was referring to a chile similar to this one: "Our dishes are all Mexican, but good ones, some are delightful; one great importance, they are well cooked; their meats are all boiled, the healthiest way of preparing them, and are in most instances cooked with vegetables."

Like many chiles, this is delicious over rice. The chicken is on the bone and cut into familiar serving pieces, which makes it a little different from other chiles, where the meat is cut into bite-sized pieces.

serves 4 to 6

One 3½- to 4-pound chicken cut into bone-in serving pieces
8 cups chicken broth, homemadeor store bought, or water
½ cup Basic Red Chile Puree, page 48
1 onion, chopped, (about 1½ cups)
3 cloves garlic, minced (about 1 tablespoon)
1½ teaspoons ground cumin
1 teaspoon dried Mexican oregano leaves
1 teaspoon kosher salt
1 sprig fresh thyme or
½ teaspoon dried thyme
1 bay leaf
1 cup dry sherry wine
½ cup drained, sliced ripe olives (2¼-ounce can)
3 tablespoons cornstarch mixed with ½ cup cold water
4 to 6 cups cooked white rice

1. In a Dutch oven or similar lidded pot, combine the chicken pieces with the broth, puree, onion, garlic, cumin, oregano, salt, thyme and bay leaf. Cover and bring to a boil over medium-high heat. Reduce the heat to low, cover, and simmer for about 30 minutes.
2. Add the sherry and olives and simmer, uncovered, for about 20 minutes or until the chicken is tender and cooked through.
3. Stir in the cornstarch mixture and continue to simmer, stirring, until the gravy thickens, about 5 minutes. Taste and adjust the seasonings. Serve over rice.

Green Chile Steak Bowl

A Green Chile Steak Bowl is a good, quick lunch. This is excellent served with a salad and a tortilla.

serves 1 to 2

1½ tablespoons unsalted butter

One 6- to 8-ounce beef tenderloin or loin strip steak, cut into bite-sized pieces

1 tablespoon all-purpose flour

1 small clove garlic, minced

½ teaspoon dried Mexican oregano leaves

1 cup beef broth, homemade or store bought

1 large poblano chile, peeled, seeded and cut in strips, or ½ cup canned mild green chiles, cut into pieces

Kosher salt

1. In a large skillet, heat the butter over medium-high heat untl it turns clear and begins to sizzle. Sauté the steak for 1 to 2 minutes, turning to brown on all sides. Push the meat to one side of the pan and sprinkle the flour over the butter and meat drippings in the pan. Stir well to make a smooth roux. Add the garlic and oregano and heat until bubbling.

2. Add the broth and stir to make a moderately thick gravy. Add the green chile pieces and cook, stirring with the meat, for about 1 minute. Season to taste with salt and serve.

How to Work with Chiles

REMOVING THE SHINY, HARD OUTER SKIN FROM A CHILE is best done by toasting it over a fire or under a broiler until the skin blisters. I roast chiles beneath an electric broiler, turning them frequently until the skin is puffed and browned. When you do this, be sure to cut off the end of the chile or pierce it so that steam can escape — otherwise you may find pieces of chile all over your oven.

Next, while they are still hot, drop the pods into a sealable plastic bag and put them in the freezer for 15 minutes. Take them from the bag and rub the loose skins off the chiles while holding them over the sink and under running cool water. Rinse and dry the peeled chile.

Do not put your fingers in your eyes or any other tender place when you handle chiles. Cover any can of chiles containing juice with a towel when you open it. I once had some chile juice made from vinegar and chile oil squirt directly into my eyes. Painful.

Corn and Bean Chile Soup

Finishing this boldly flavored chile soup with a topping of mild cheese has probably been common practice for generations. Yet Susan Shelby Magoffin was dismissive of the cheeses she encountered in 1847 as she traveled the Santa Fe Trail, clearly missing the cheeses she had grown up eating in Kentucky. "Their cheese is clabber," she wrote of New Mexican cheese, "and made on the same principle as the Dutch smerecase though very tough, mean looking, and to me, unpalatable."

serves 8 to 10

2 cups (16-ounces) pinto beans

2 cups fresh corn, cut from the cobs, or canned or frozen corn kernels

1 onion, chopped (about 1½ cups)

1 large clove garlic, minced

¾ cup Basic Red Chile Puree, page 48

2 to 3 teaspoons dried Mexican oregano leaves

2 teaspoons kosher salt

1 teaspoon ground cumin

8 to 10 large fried bread croutons, optional, see Note

1½ cups crumbled goat cheese or Monterey Jack cheese

1. Pick over the beans and soak in 2 quarts of cold water to cover for at least 8 hours or overnight. Alternatively, pour 2 quarts of boiling water over the beans, cover, and soak for 1 hour.
2. Rinse and drain the beans and put them in a large Dutch oven or similar pot. Add 2 quarts of cold water to the pot and bring to a boil over medium-high heat. Reduce the heat to low, cover, and simmer, stirring occasionally, for 2½ to 3 hours or until the beans are tender. If the beans seem dry, add some hot water.
3. Stir the corn, onion, garlic, chile puree, oregano, salt, and cumin into the beans. Let the beans return to a simmer, cover, and cook for 50 to 60 minutes.
4. Serve bowls of the hot soup topped with crisp fried bread croutons, if desired, and sprinkled with cheese.

Note: The croutons are easy to make. Slice a slender loaf of French bread into rounds about 1-inch thick. In a skillet, heat about ½ inch of olive oil over medium-high heat and when hot, fry the bread slices until golden brown on both sides. Turn once during frying. If you would rather bake the croutons, brush the slices with olive oil, arrange them on a baking sheet, and bake in a preheated 375°F. oven for 6 to 8 minutes, turning once, until golden brown.

CHAPTER 4

A Trinity Of Indian Foods

CORN, BEANS, AND SQUASH COMPRISE THE TRINITY OF Native American foods, often called the Three Sacred Sisters. Corn provided the Indians with food and drink. The husks were woven into baskets to store food and other things. Beans, too, were a staple that were eaten all year long, and squash, so easy to grow, provided sustenance as well as vessels for eating and storing food.

Plains Indians used very few spices — even salt was rare. Roasted coltsfoot herb was used in place of salt but most of the food featured only the flavor of corn, beans, squash and meat.

Mohawk Indian Corn

The Plains Indians often dry the corn right on the cob and later, when they are ready to eat the corn, soak the cobs overnight in water. The hydrated corn kernels taste almost as good as fresh.

The native people of the Southwest sometimes steam the corn and then dry the kernels. These are called chicos or little ones. Chicos also are soaked for long hours and then used stews, vegetable mixtures and any other dish that calls for corn.

Popcorn is not new. More than 5,000 years ago, the Indians in Mexico popped corn and strung it for religious ceremonies. Even today, in remote Mexican churches one sometimes finds the statues of the Virgin or Christ decorated with strings of popcorn.

In George Herter's book, Bull Cook and Authentic Historical Recipes and Practices, *is a recipe for Mohawk Indian Corn. While this may not be authentic, Mr. Herter's claims that the corn flavor is wonderfully amplified and improved by the addition of black walnut flavoring and black walnuts is true. It really is delicious.*

serves 4 to 6

3 cups fresh, frozen, or canned whole kernel corn (no need to drain if using canned corn)

½ cup black walnut halves or pieces (use English walnuts if you can't find black walnuts)

2 to 3 tablespoons unsalted butter

½ teaspoon black walnut flavoring, see Note

Kosher salt and freshly ground black pepper

1. Put the corn in a saucepan. If using canned corn, include the juices. Stir in the black walnuts and enough water to cover the corn. Bring to a simmer over medium heat.
2. Add the butter and black walnut flavoring, stir to mix and continue to simmer until the butter melts. Season to taste with salt and pepper and serve.

Note: Black walnut flavoring, also called extract, is sold in many supermarkets and specialty markets. It is available in stores that primarily sell spices, and also can be bought on line.

Blue Indian Cornmeal Tamale Pie

Many Indians and Southwesterners still cook with the blue cornmeal ground from the dark-hued Indian corn called maiz axul (blue corn). The cornmeal is most often used for tortillas, and it's magnificent in this old recipe for tamale pie.

serves 8 to 10

2 cups blue or yellow cornmeal

Salt

6 tablespoons all purpose flour, divided

2 to 4 tablespoons olive or corn oil

2 pounds ground beef, buffalo, or game meat

1 cup chopped yellow onion (1 small onion)

1 clove garlic, chopped

1 teaspoon dried Mexican oregano leaves, crushed

2 to 3 tablespoons ground New Mexican red chile or 2 cups fresh or canned chopped green chiles

One 14½-ounce can diced tomatoes with jalapeños

1 cup pitted ripe olives, sliced, optional

3 cups grated Monterey Jack and Colby cheeses (about 12 ounces of cheese)

1. In a mixing bowl, stir together the cornmeal, 2 cups of cold water, and 2 teaspoons of salt.

2. In a large, heavy Dutch oven with a lid, bring 6 cups of water to a boil over medium heat. Slowly pour the cornmeal mixture into the boiling water, stirring as you do, reduce the heat to low and cook, stirring constantly, until the mixture thickens. Cover and cook over very low heat, stirring frequently, for about 30 minute or until the mixture is very thick and mush-like.

3. Sprinkle 4 tablespoons of flour over the mush and whisk or stir until thoroughly combined. Cook, stirring, for 2 to 3 minutes to cook the flour.

4. Lightly oil the bottom and sides of a 9-by-12-by-2½-inch baking dish. Spoon half the cornmeal mush into the dish and spread in an even layer. Refrigerate until needed.

5. Preheat the oven to 350°F.

6. Coat a large frying pan with oil and set over medium-high heat. When hot, fry the beef, onion, garlic, and oregano, stirring and breaking up the beef until it is lightly browned. Add the ground red chile or chopped green chile, stir in the remaining 2 tablespoons of flour. Cook for 1 to 2 minutes, stirring to mix well.

7. Add the tomatoes and 1½ cups of water. Cook, stirring, over medium-low heat for about 5 minutes to make a medium-thick gravy. Stir in the olive slices, taste and season with salt. Let the mixture cool for at least 15 minutes.

8. Remove the baking dish from the refrigerator and sprinkle 1 cup of cheese over the chilled mush. Spoon the meat mixture over the cheese and sprinkle with 1 cup of cheese. Top with the remaining mush, smooth the top with a spatula, and top with the remaining cup of cheese.

9. Bake for until the mixture is heated all the way through and is bubbling, 40 to 50 minutes. Allow the baked pie to sit for 15 to 20 minutes to firm up before serving.

Posole with Pork and Red Chile

In New England, ground cornmeal was called samp and in the South it was hominy. The Indians of Mexico and New Mexico call it nixtamal. The same cornmeal can also be toasted and used in a wide variety of ways: as pinole, chaquehue, champurrado, and was-nah.

When cool weather comes to New Mexico, a favorite dish for parties and family get-togethers is made with posole (sometimes spelled pozole), which is a form of hominy. Although hominy in its commercial, canned state is rather dull and bland, when prepared as Native Americans do, with meats and herbs, it is magnificent.

serves 10 to 12

2 cups dry posole, 2 pounds frozen posole, or two 29-ounce cans Mexican-style hominy

3 to 4 tablespoons olive or corn oil

2 pounds pork shoulder, cut into bite-sized pieces

1 yellow onion, chopped (about 1½ cups)

3 garlic cloves, minced (about 1 tablespoon)

12 cups chicken or beef broth or water

1 cup Basic Red Chile Puree, page 48

1½ teaspoons kosher salt

1 teaspoon leaf oregano

½ teaspoon cumin

Sliced avocado, shredded Monterey Jack cheese, and sour cream, for garnish

Flour tortillas

1. If using dry posole: Rinse the posole in cold water until the water runs clear and then soak it in cold water to cover for at least 8 hours. Drain and put the posole in a large pot and add cold water to cover. Bring to a boil over medium-high heat, reduce the heat to low and simmer, covered, until the kernels pops, about 1 hour.

2. If using frozen posole: Thaw it, at least partially, and then put the posole in a pot and add enough water to cover by 2 inches. Lightly salt the water and bring to a boil over medium-high heat. Reduce the heat and simmer over medium heat for about 45 minutes, until the kernels pop.

3. If using Mexican-style canned hominy: Drain the hominy and rinse it under cold water, before adding it to the soup or stew.

4. In a large Dutch oven or similar heavy-bottomed pot, heat the oil over medium heat. Add the pork and brown, turning with tongs, until lightly browned on all sides. Do not crowd the pot. If necessary brown the meat in batches. Remove the pork with a slotted spoon and set aside.

5. Add the onion and garlic, and cook, stirring until the onion softens and is lightly browned, about 5 minutes. Take care not to burn the garlic by reducing the heat, if necessary. Stir in the broth, chile puree, salt, oregano, and cumin.

6. Add the posole to the pot and bring to a boil over medium-high heat. Reduce the heat to low, cover, and simmer for 2 to 3 hours, stirring occasionally, until the pork and hominy are tender and the flavors have blended. Adjust the heat up or down during cooking to maintain the simmer.

7. Taste and adjust seasonings. Spoon the posole into bowls and serve with the suggested toppings and warm flour tortillas.

Frijoles

The beans the Indians used came in many forms. There were red and black beans, spotted pintos, and brown bolito beans. Alongside these were the more familiar kidney, lima and navy beans.

Pinto beans, also called frijoles, were and still are a staple of the Western diet — and when well cooked are some of the best eating anywhere. It's a shame that beans have earned a reputation for being a poor man's food; they are high in protein, very nourishing and nothing short of delicious. To cook them is simple enough.

Old time cooks soaked dried beans overnight in cold water to hydrate them, a method that works very well, but if you are in a hurry, there is a more modern way called the quick-soak method. Rinse and pick over the beans (to get rid of any small stones or other detritus) and put the beans in a large pot. Pour 10 cups of boiling water over the beans, cover the pot, and let them soak for 1 hour. Drain the beans, which are now ready to cook.

serves 8 to 10

2 cups (16 ounces) dried pinto bean

3 strips bacon or ¼ pound salt pork, cubed

Kosher salt

½ cup Red Chile Puree, page 48, optional

1. In a large pot, add enough water to the beans to cover by 2 inches. Add the bacon or salt pork and bring to a boil over high heat. As soon as the water boils, reduce the heat and simmer over medium or medium-low heat for 2 to 3 hours or until the beans are tender. Adjust the heat up or down to maintain a slow simmer. If you must add additional water, make sure it is hot water; cold water will toughen the beans.
2. Season the beans to taste with salt. Stir the chile puree into the beans, if using, and serve.

★ BEFORE METAL KETTLES

We were able to film a resourceful Native American technique for using a beef paunch as an edible cooking vessel in Rosebud, South Dakota, in 1969. An old Brule Sioux named Carl Ironshell took the washed paunch, or stomach, from a newly killed steer and hung it from four, forked posts that had been driven into the ground. The paunch was suspended, spread out between the posts, each corner hooked over the forked ends. Once it was in place, about three gallons of water were poured into the paunch along with several pounds of raw beef, chopped into bite-sized pieces.

As this was going on, smooth river rocks were being heated in a hot, wood fire burning nearby. When the rocks were hot, they were transferred to the paunch to heat the water. By the time the fifth rock was dropped in the water, it was boiling furiously. The rocks were removed, heated and returned to the paunch and after about an hour, the meat was cooked and the broth was steaming and ready.

Following this repast, the paunch itself was eaten; mainly uncooked. It is not a dish to delight the fastidious gourmet, but interesting nonetheless. It highlights the ingenuity of the Indian cooks, who used whatever materials were available for cooking.

Baked Stuffed Pumpkin

Squash comes in many varieties and every Native American house usually has a storage area where chunks of dried squash, and other foodstuffs, are kept. The most familiar American squash is the pumpkin and this dish is based on a traditional Indian recipe for baked pumpkin. They used a lot of toasted sunflower seeds in their food, which gives this stew a distinctive flavor. Bring out your favorite hot sauce as a condiment to serve with this.

serves 6 to 8

1 (4- to 5-pound) sugar pumpkin
2 tablespoons unsalted butter, melted
Fine sea salt, to taste
Coarsely ground black pepper, to taste
2 tablespoons olive oil
2 cups chopped white onion (1 large)
1 pound ground buffalo or lean ground beef
2 cups fresh corn kernels
or 1 can (11 ounces) white shoepeg corn, drained
2 cups fresh green beans
1 cup chopped green bell pepper
1 cup diced, cooked chicken
1 cup hulled sunflower seeds
4 cups chicken broth
2 fresh peaches, peeled, pitted, and sliced
Hot pepper sauce, optional

1. Preheat the oven to 350°F.

2. With a large, sharp knife, cut the top off the pumpkin jack-o'-lantern style. With a large spoon, scrape out the seeds and strings (save the seeds to salt and bake for a snack). Rub the inside of the pumpkin generously with melted butter, and season with salt and pepper. Place the pumpkin in a roasting pan. Bake, with the top off, for about 45 minutes, or until the pumpkin is tender, but still holds its shape. Check after 30 minutes for liquid buildup. Using a long handled ladle, remove any juice, and discard. The pumpkin may collapse while baking if you don't remove the liquid.

3. Meanwhile, in a Dutch oven or heavy-bottomed sauté pan, heat the olive oil. Add the onion and cook over medium heat until translucent, about 5 minutes. Add buffalo and sauté until browned, 6 to 8 minutes. Stir in the corn, green beans, bell pepper, diced chicken, sunflower seeds, chicken broth, and peaches. When the liquid comes to a boil, reduce the heat to low and simmer the stew gently, for about 10 minutes to blend the flavors.

4. Carefully lift the baked pumpkin onto a round, serving platter. Ladle the stew into the pumpkin and top with the lid. As you serve, be sure to scrape the inside of the pumpkin to mix some of its delicious flesh into the stew.

Was-Nah, Indian Version

Plains Indians generally relied on berries for dessert, although corn, with its natural sweetness, could be toasted, too. A broad term for a toasted corn dessert is Was-Nah and sometimes you'll find a Sioux who calls a type of pemmican Was-Nah. An older Sioux lady friend named Loves Horses taught me this recipe. An updated recipe follows. Warn your guests that with the pits, this will have a gritty texture.

serves 16 to 18

1 cup fresh, unpitted choke cherries

1½ cups yellow cornmeal

¼ pound buffalo or beef kidney fat

½ to ¾ cup brown sugar

1. Preheat the oven to 350°F.

2. Pound the cherries in a stone mortar to crush the fruit and its pits.

3. Spread the cornmeal in an even layer in a shallow baking pan and toast it on the middle rack of the oven for about 20 minutes or until lightly browned. Watch closely and stir the cornmeal several times so that it toasts evenly.

4. Using a meat grinder, grind the kidney fat. This fat is the best and purest found on an animal.

5. In a saucepan, heat the fat over medium heat until it renders (melts). Add the fat to the toasted cornmeal and stir in the brown sugar. Add the cherries and mash everything together.

6. Chill the Was-Nah until it is firm. Give each person a heaping tablespoon.

Was-Nah, Modern Version

The toasted meal has something of the flavor of popped corn. With the butter, sugar and cherries, it is simply delicious. This version is a little more palatable for contemporary palates than the preceding one.

serves 16 to 18

1½ cups pitted fresh or frozen tart cherries or Bing cherries

1½ cups yellow cornmeal, toasted (as described on page 70)

¼ to ¾ cup brown sugar

½ cup (1 stick) unsalted butter, melted

1. Put the cherries through a food mill or chop in the bowl of a food processor fitted with the metal blade.

2. In a bowl, mix together the cherries, cornmeal, sugar, and butter. Chill until firm.

Baked Indian Pudding

Elizabeth Burt, whose Fort Laramie Chicken Salad is on page 30, had a recipe in her cookbook for baked pudding. It is a rich, heavy pudding and I prefer to garnish it with lightly sweetened whipped cream, rather than the sugared butter Elizabeth recommends.

serves 10 to 12

4 cups milk
2 cups yellow cornmeal
1 cup unsulfured molasses
2 tablespoons unsalted butter
3 large eggs
Grated zest of 1 large lemon
1½ cups raisins and/or sweetened dried cranberries
2 cups lightly sweetened whipped cream

1. Preheat the oven to 325°F. Butter a 9- by 12-inch baking dish.

2. In a large measuring cup, whisk together 1 cup of the milk, 1 cup of water and the cornmeal.

3. In a large saucepan bring the remaining 3 cups of milk to a boil over medium heat. Reduce the heat to low and slowly pour the cornmeal mixture into the boiling milk, stirring constantly for about 5 minutes or until the mixture is smooth and thickened. Remove from the heat and set aside.

4. In a small saucepan, heat the molasses and the butter until the butter melts. Stir together.

5. In a large mixing bowl, whisk the eggs well. Gradually whisk in the molasses mixture and then stir in the cornmeal mixture, lemon zest, and dried fruit.

6. Pour the pudding into the prepared baking dish and smooth the top. Cover tightly with aluminum foil and then put the dish in a larger pan. Pour enough hot water into the pan to come halfway up the side the baking dish. Bake for about 1½ hours or until the pudding has the texture of firm custard. Let the pudding cool for about 30 minutes before serving.

7. Cut the pudding into squares and serve topped with whipped cream.

CHAPTER 5

Bread of the Frontier

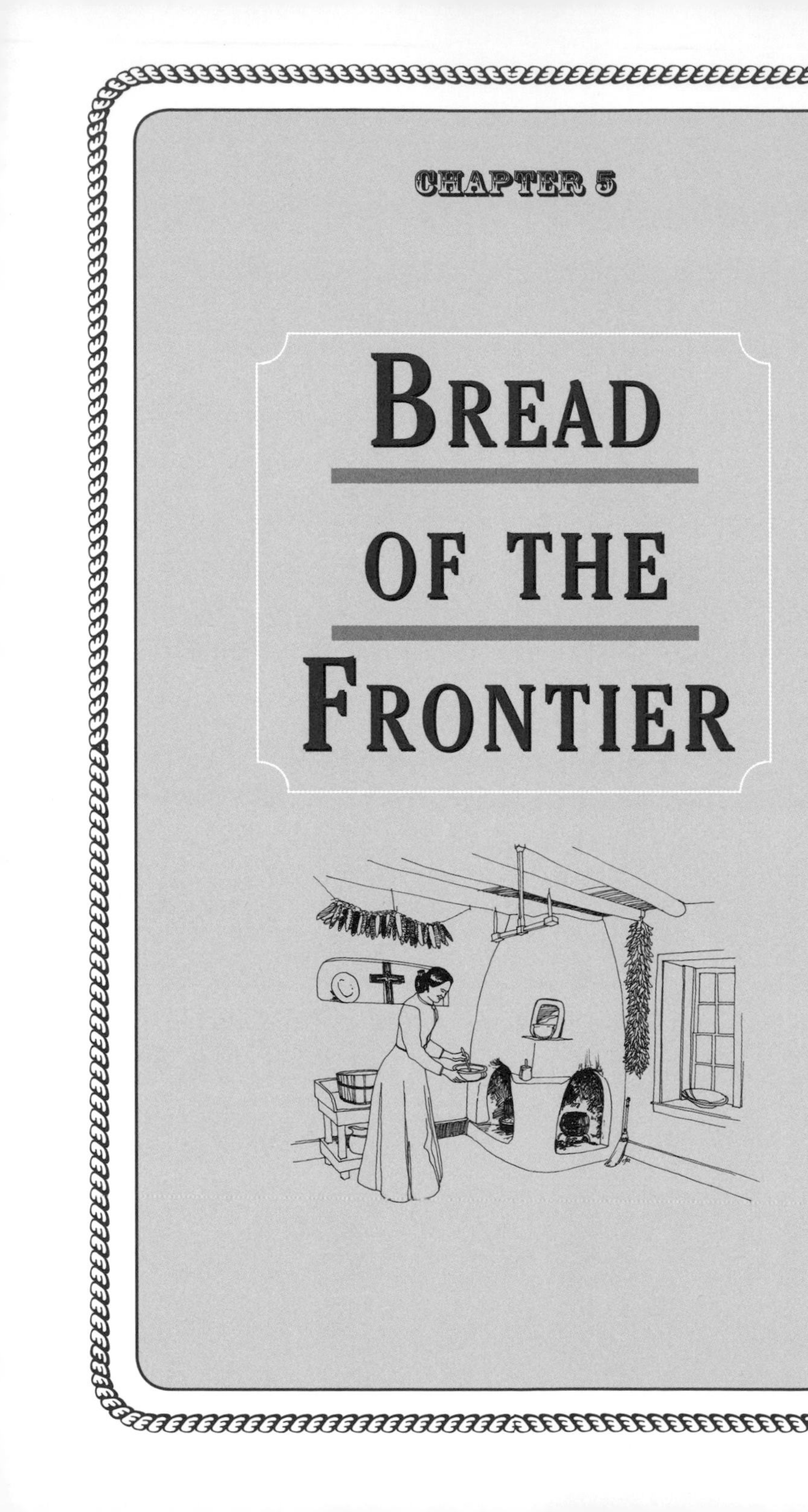

FROM THE ATLANTIC COAST WESTWARD, STOMACHS were nourished by a Native American grass, which we call corn. Many varieties of corn exist. Among the smallest is the three-inch-long ear of raspberry corn — the kernels look like popcorn but are scarlet— and among the biggest are the large hybrid cobs of golden kernels we know so well today.

From prehistoric times, the grain served as the basic ration of Indian peoples, and was eagerly adopted by the frontiersmen as a basic foodstuff. A handful of cornmeal kept in an animal bladder was the "iron ration" of the Indian warrior. In addition to cornmeal for cornbread, frontiersmen, Native Americans, and others depended on wheat flour, potatoes, and yeast to make bread — always necessary for subsistence.

Old-Fashioned Potato Bread

Elizabeth Burt's recipe journal, From Fort Laramie, *is a treasure trove, describing the foods cooked and enjoyed during the time of the troubled times of the Indian Wars. Mrs. Burt's recipe for potato bread inspired this hearty, but light textured recipe.*

makes 3 loaves

4 small to medium russet (Idaho) potatoes
Two ¼-ounce packages active dry yeast
½ cup sugar
½ cup lukewarm (105° to 115°F) water
3 large eggs, beaten until blended
1 tablespoon kosher salt
½ cup softened unsalted butter or vegetable shortening
5 to 7 cups bread flour
Shortening or vegetable oil, for greasing pans

1. Boil the potatoes in enough water to cover by 2 inches, until tender, 25 to 30 minutes. Drain the potato cooking water into a large measuring cup and set it aside to cool until tepid. Peel the potatoes and either press the flesh through a ricer, or mash them with a fork. Measure out 1 cup of the mashed potatoes to use in the bread, and reserve the rest for another use.

2. In a large mixing bowl, dissolve the yeast with 1 tablespoon of sugar in the lukewarm water. Let stand for 5 to 10 minutes, until the yeast bubbles and foams. With a large wooden spoon, stir in the eggs, 1½ cups of tepid potato water, salt, remaining sugar, mashed potatoes, and butter. Continue to mix with the wooden spoon, or transfer to a large electric mixer with a dough hook.

3. Gradually add enough flour, kneading by hand or with the dough hook, until dough that is smooth, elastic, but still sticky.

4. Turn the dough out onto a lightly floured surface and continue to knead by hand, adding more flour as needed, until the dough is as smooth as a baby's bottom. Put the kneaded dough in a large greased mixing bowl and turn once to coat the top. Cover the bowl with a clean, damp, dish towel and set aside in a warm, draft-free place to rise until the dough has doubled in size, about 1 hour.

5. Grease the bottom and sides of 3 medium (8½- by 4¼-inch) loaf pans. Punch down the dough and turn it out onto the lightly floured surface. Divide it into 3 equal portions. Pat a portion of dough into a rough rectangle and roll it out to a thickness of about 2 inches to work out any air bubbles. Roll up the dough, pinching the edges and shaping it. Put it in the prepared loaf pan seam-side-down. Repeat with the remaining dough and pans. Cover the loaf pans with a clean, damp, kitchen towel and allow loaves to rise in a warm, draft-free place until doubled, 35 to 45 minutes.

6. Preheat the oven to 400°F.

7. Put the loaves on the middle rack of the oven. Bake for 5 minutes and then reduce the oven temperature to 350°F. Continue to bake the loaves for 20 to 30 minutes until they are nicely browned and there is a hollow sound when you lightly tap the top of the loaf.

8. Put the pans on a rack to cool. After 30 minutes, run a knife around the edges of the pans, turn out the loaves and put them back on the rack to cool completely.

Skillet Cornbread

Cornbread is an American favorite, baked in the ovens of New England, the Deep South and the Western plains. It was often baked and served from a heavy, black cast-iron skillet because just about every cook had such a skillet and it could easily transfer from stovetop to oven.

serves 4 to 6

6 strips lean bacon

2 cups yellow, white or blue cornmeal

1 tablespoon sugar

1½ teaspoons kosher salt

1½ teaspoons baking soda (2 teaspoons at sea level)

1¼ cups buttermilk

2 large eggs

¼ cup chopped green onions, white and green parts

1. In an 8- or 9-inch heavy iron skillet (it needs to be oven safe), cook the bacon until crisp over medium-low heat. Remove the bacon, drain on paper towels, crumble, and set aside. Reserve the drippings in the skillet.
2. Preheat the oven to 350°F.
3. In a large mixing bowl, stir together the cornmeal, sugar, salt, and baking soda.
4. In a separate bowl, beat together 1 tablespoon of the reserved bacon drippings, buttermilk, and eggs.
5. Heat the skillet over medium heat, rotating to coat well with the remaining drippings. Stir the wet ingredients into the dry ones and fold in the bacon and green onions. Pour the batter into the preheated skillet and bake for about 30 minutes, until a knife inserted in the center of the bread comes out clean and the top is golden brown. Cut in wedges and serve directly from the skillet.

★ PIKI BREAD, FOOD FOR THE GODS

Piki is the name for an interesting version of cornbread still found among the Indians of Arizona. These are rolls of crisp, tissue-thin cornbread, rolled up like a morning newspaper. The early Spanish called these crispy loaves guayabes, perhaps because they resemble guavas.

Pikis are made by spreading a thin gruel made from corn and sage on a hot rock, where it cooks almost instantaneously. The moment the bread is cooked, it's peeled from the rock and rolled up tightly. The breads may be colored with native yellow saffron or with red cockscomb, but the most common color is a blue-black, made from blue Indian corn. Brightly colored pikis, fastened together, are known as Kachina, food for the gods.

Lakota Indian Fry Bread

This recipe relies on basic bread dough leavened with baking powder. The dough is formed into flat rectangles or disks and cooked in hot lard. The process is quick and uncomplicated and the crispy light bread makes a marvelous treat. These are served with honey or cinnamon sugar for a sweet treat, although without either, the breads can be used with savory preparations such as dips or soups. Whatever your pleasure, the most important thing about fry bread is that it must be eaten hot, immediately after it's cooked.

serves 4 to 6; makes about 20 pieces of bread

1 quart tallow, lard, or canola oil, for deep frying
1¾ cups all-purpose flour, plus more for rolling out
1½ teaspoons baking powder
¾ teaspoon salt
Honey or cinnamon sugar, for serving

1. Heat the oil in a deep pot to 380°F. The best flavor comes from either beef tallow (rendered beef fat) or lard, but canola oil works, too.

2. The easiest way to make fry bread is with a dough hook attachment on an electric mixer. In the mixer bowl, thoroughly combine the flour, baking powder, and salt. Add ¾ cup water and mix until a supple, uniform dough forms. Add more water if needed to achieve a dough that is not too sticky but not too dry.

3. Divide the dough into 4 to 6 equal portions, and form into rounds. Roll out the rounds on a floured surface to a thickness of between ½ and ¼ inch.

4. If you'd like to try Pueblo-style fry bread, use your finger to make a ¾-inch hole in the center of each piece of dough. If you don't have a thermometer to check the heat of the oil, carefully lower a small piece of dough into the hot oil. It should blister and puff up instantly. In the first few seconds of frying, use a spoon to pour fat over the bread to make sure all surfaces fry immediately. Remove and drain on a paper towel. Allow a full minute between batches to bring the oil back up to temperature.

5. Many people dip dry bread in honey or bite a hole in the side and squeeze honey into the center. Others sprinkle cinnamon sugar on it.

The Taste of Mexico

THAT MARVELOUS TASTE FOUND IN MODERN CORN chips, such as Fritos, tortilla chips, taco shells and other Mexican-style corn products, comes not from a particular type of corn, but rather from how the cornmeal is processed. When the corn kernels' hard covering is removed with slaked lime caustics, a residual scent remains. This is slightly musty and contains hints of lime, even after the corn has been washed numerous times. These factors contribute to the unmistakable flavor. When the corn is dried and ground into meal, it is called nixtamal and imparts the inimitable flavor of Mexican food to all it is used with.

When the meal, or masa, is mixed with water and a little salt and griddled into thin cakes, the result is a tortilla — the beloved flat bread of Mexico and the Southwest. Tortillas also may be made with wheat flour and these, usually larger and lighter colored tortillas, are used for burritos. Navajo and Hopi Indians add a bit of wood ash to the masa for balls of cornmeal, which are cooked in a fire's coals for little walnut-sized bread rolls.

Blue cornmeal, also called Hopi corn, is made by grinding the blue corn grown in the Southwest. It is produced by a number of mills — more every year — and makes the very best corn tortillas.

Bannock Bread

The term "Bannock" is used by different Native American tribes to describe slightly different breads. The Bannock, or Banate, people of southern Idaho and western Wyoming traditionally wore their hair in a topknot that reminded early white settlers of a loaf of bannock.

serves 6

⅓ cup melted unsalted butter

2 cups all-purpose flour

2 teaspoons baking powder (reduce to 1½ teaspoons or 1 teaspoon at high altitudes)

½ teaspoon salt

2½ teaspoons sugar

⅓ cup sweetened dried cranberries

⅓ cup dried blueberries or currants

¾ cup milk

1. Preheat the oven to 350°F. Brush the bottom and sides of a heavy, 9-inch ovenproof iron skillet or 8- to 9-inch shallow baking pan with butter. Reserve remaining butter.

2. Sift the flour, baking powder, and salt into a medium mixing bowl. Stir in the sugar and dried fruit. Add the milk and the remaining butter, and stir with a wooden spatula to form a moist, but not sticky dough. Gently press the dough into the buttered skillet. Bake on the middle rack of the oven for about 30 minutes, until the loaf is golden brown. Serve bannock warm with sweet butter.

CHAPTER 6

FRONTIER DESSERTS

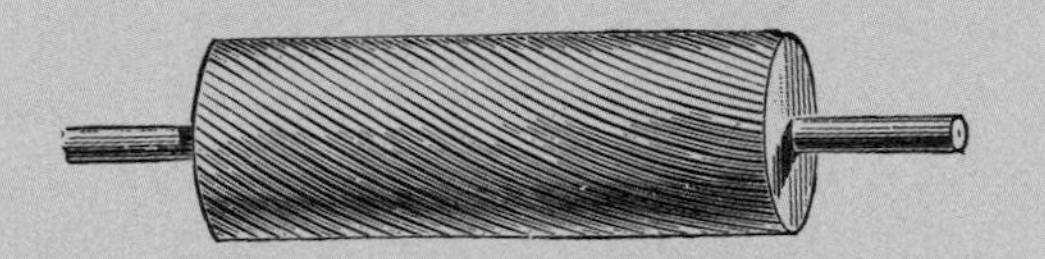

MAN SEEMS TO HAVE A SWEET TOOTH, NO MATTER WHERE he comes from. The habit of having a sweet item for dessert was well known among the Europeans and not unknown to the Indians. New Mexicans, who are a cultural mixture of Spanish and Native American, found that fruits with their natural sugars were the most readily available source of sweetness. Although cane sugar and molasses were well known in the early West (coming from the Caribbean and from Mexico), they were luxuries that had to travel a long way on wagons. And yet, all the early fur trade forts had molasses, or "long sweet," as it was then called, on hand.

Chess Pie

Southerners carried this everyday pie with them when they moved west. Probably of English origin, it is one of the simplest and best pies you can bake. Where does it get its name? By most accounts, it is a formalization of the term "jes pie" — which most likely was how many home cooks referred to this blending of ingredients every household had on hand most of the time.

serves 4 to 6

¾ cup sugar
2 tablespoons unsalted butter, softened
4 large eggs
Finely grated zest and juice of 1 large or 2 small lemons
⅛ teaspoon salt
One 8-inch pie shell, lightly baked and cooled (see page 87)

1. Preheat the oven to 350°F.
2. Put the sugar, butter, eggs, zest, and salt in a blender. Cut the lemon in half and use a small sharp knife to cut between the sections and scoop out the pulp. Put the pulp in the blender and squeeze any remaining juice from the lemon into the blender. Pulse on and off until well combined.
3. Spoon or pour the filling into the cooled pie shell. Smooth the surface and bake for 25 to 35 minutes, until the crust is nicely browned, and the filling seems set in the center when the pie plate is jiggled.
4. Allow the pie to cool on a wire rack before serving. Refrigerate the cooled pie, if not serving immediately.

Pies and Tarts

MANY RECIPES ON THESE PAGES CALL FOR A PRE-baked, or blind baked, pie shell. To do so, prick the dough — which you can make from a favorite recipe or buy already made from the supermarket — on the bottom of the pie shell with the tines of fork. Cover it with a circle of baking parchment or aluminum foil. Pour pie weights, uncooked rice, or dried beans into the pie shell to weight the parchment or foil.

Bake the pie shell in a preheated 450°F. oven for 10 to 15 minutes. Remove the shell from the oven and carefully remove the weights and paper or foil. Let the pie crust cool — it is now ready to be filled

According to Stuart Berg Flexner, a noted scholar of the American language and American social history, the word "pie" meant a meat pie to both the English and the first colonists. These folks used the word "tart" when referring to a pastry filled with fruit, berries, or jam. Nonetheless, the colonists were soon calling both sweet and savory pastry dishes "pies" and ate both for breakfast.

The word "pie" can be traced back to "pica," the Latin word for magpie, a bird that fills its nest with miscellaneous objects. One could argue that the English do the same when filling meat pies.

Transparent Pie

The recipes for chess pies and chess cakes were all pretty much the same. If the cook had some type of sharp jelly or preserves on hand, they might dollop a big spoonful in the center of the pie. This one, with a cup of red currant jelly in the mix, is a typical chess pie, also called "transparent pie." Why transparent? It's an old-fashioned term for pies made without the addition of fruit or nuts. It does not mean you can see through the filling. Mrs. William Shannon of Broomfield, Colorado, provided us with her variation for one of these homespun pies, with a recipe that came from Virginia-Kentucky frontier period. It's easy and delicious.

serves 6 to 8

1 cup red currant jelly

One 9-inch pie shell, lightly baked and cooled (see page 87)

1 cup sugar

½ cup (1 stick) unsalted butter, melted

½ cup heavy cream

4 large eggs, beaten

2 tablespoons all-purpose flour

1 teaspoon pure vanilla extract

⅛ teaspoon kosher salt

1. Preheat the oven to 375°F. Position a rack in the center of the oven.
2. In the top of a double boiler or small saucepan set over a larger pot of simmering water, melt the currant jelly until liquefied. Spread a layer of jelly in the bottom of the pie shell.
3. In a mixing bowl, mix together the sugar and melted butter. Add the cream, eggs, flour, vanilla, and salt and whisk until well blended. Pour the custard over the jelly.
4. Bake the pie on the middle rack for about 40 minutes, or until the top is puffed and golden brown, and the filling seems set in the middle when the pie plate is jiggled.
5. Allow pie to cool on a rack before serving. Refrigerate the cooled pie, if not serving immediately.

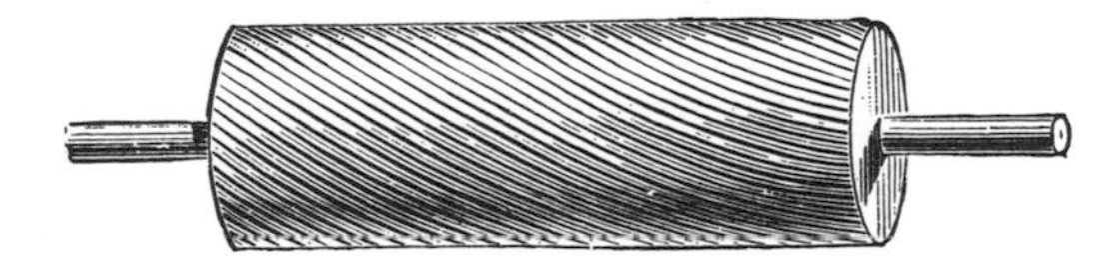

Apple Pie Without Apples

At Fort Robinson, Nebraska, the famous old cavalry headquarters, I found a recipe for an apple pie with no apples, which demonstrates the ingenuity of the early frontier cooks. It is a very good dish and with the exception of the absence of seeds, you almost can't tell it from real apple pie.

serves 6 to 8

Dough for two 9-inch prepared, unbaked pie crusts

20 soda (saltine) crackers

Juice of 1 lemon

2 large eggs

1 cup sugar or ½ cup honey

1 cup milk

1¼ teaspoons grated nutmeg

¾ teaspoon ground cinnamon

Finely grated zest of 1 lemon

1. Preheat the oven to 350°F. Position a rack in the center of the oven. Fit 1 of the pie crusts into a 9-inch pie plate, pressing it over the bottom and up the sides of the pie plate.

2. Break up the soda crackers, toss them with the lemon juice and put them in the pie plate.

3. In a mixing bowl (or blender), whisk together the eggs, sugar or honey, milk, nutmeg, cinnamon, and lemon zest. Pour over the crackers and lay the top crust over the pie. Crimp the edges of the dough so that the top and bottom crusts are sealed. Prick a few small holes in the top crust to allow steam to escape during baking.

4. Bake on the middle rack of the oven for about 1 hour, until the crust is golden brown. Let the pie cool slightly on a wire rack before slicing.

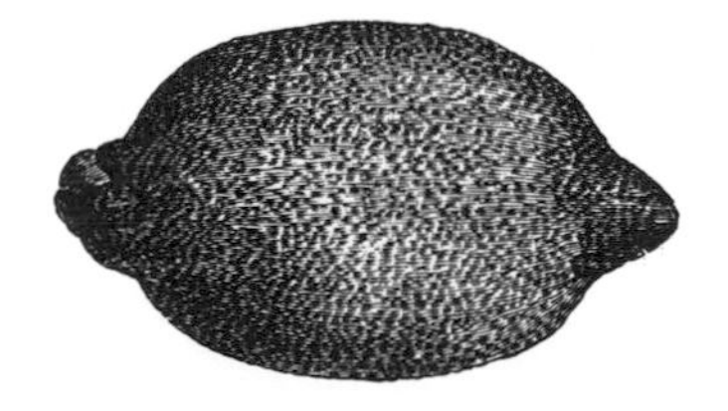

White Eyes Wo-Japi

On the Sioux Indian reservation, the old people still make a dessert called Wo-Japi, pronounced whoa-zha-pee. They mash ripe choke cherries into small cakes from the berries and allow them to dry. Later, when these are to be used, the Indians soak the cakes in water until soft. At this point, they use a stone mallet to mash the cakes. The mashed cake(s) is put in a kettle with flour and sugar and cooked into a dessert, thickened by the flour and sweetened with the sugar. An easier and less chewy version is below.

serves 8 to 10

4 cups fresh or frozen boysenberries or blackberries
2 cups sugar
4 tablespoons all-purpose flour
Grated zest and juice of 1 lemon
Lightly sweetened whipped cream or ice cream, optional

1. Put the berries and sugar in a large saucepan and add 1½ cups of water. Cook over medium heat until the berries soften and the sugar melts.
2. In a small bowl, whisk the flour and about ½ cup cold water to a smooth thin paste.
3. When the fruit comes to a simmer, stir in the flour paste, lemon zest and juice and, still stirring, bring to a boil over medium heat until the flour loses its raw flavor, about 15 minutes.
4. Remove from the heat, let the mixture cool, and when room temperature, refrigerate until cold or for up to 4 days. Serve cold with whipped cream or ice cream, if desired.

Capirotada

or Spotted Dog Bread Pudding

CAPIROTADA IS A FAVORITE, OLD DESSERT FROM NEW Mexico that began as a savory dish of layered bread, onions, meat and cheese. It eventually turned sweet and became much loved in the Southwest and Mexico, where it was a Lenten dish.

New Mexico was cut off from the rest of Mexico primarily by distance and in the early days, the missions were supplied by wagon trains, which brought wines, fruit, seeds for trees, and shoots for grape vines. The wagons also brought chocolate, cheeses, and delicacies from Europe, which were meant for the French or Spanish priests. It is quite likely that the many apple orchards still standing in New Mexico grew from these seeds. These same apples made their way into capirotada, along with bread, raisins, brown sugar, cinnamon, and nutmeg, as well as Cheddar cheese and some long-cooked onions.

When the early mountain men encountered capirotada, they insisted on calling it "spotted dog" because of the raisins dotting the pudding, and because it was easier to remember than capirotada. Spotted dog is such a colorful name that later, chuck wagon cooks made a variation of the dessert that they dubbed "spotted pup."

Cider-Cooked Trappers' Fruit

It comes as no surprise that both the early trappers and soldiers, as well as the Native Americans, relied heavily on dried fruits to get them through the winter. The fruits were accompanied by other dried foods such as buffalo jerky and fat, and gathered nuts, all survival foods. Indians often subsisted on a mixture of fat, dried meat, nuts, and fruits called pemmican, and while it may not appeal to our modern palates, it was a nutritious substitute for a substantial meal; traders, trappers, and the army often turned to pemmican, too. This dried fruit compote is delicious spooned over ice cream and also can accompany meat. As the dried apples, spices, hazelnuts, and rum cook, the compote just turns more syrupy, mellow, dark, and delicious.

serves 8

4 quarts apple cider
2 pounds dried apples
2 cups applesauce
½ cup fresh lemon juice (juice of 2 lemons)
½ cup golden raisins
3 tablespoons brown sugar or honey
1 tablespoon coriander seeds
1 tablespoon pure vanilla extract
½ teaspoon ground cinnamon
½ teaspoon ground cloves
½ teaspoon grated nutmeg
½ cup lightly toasted, coarsely chopped hazelnuts
1 cup Meyer's rum

1. In a large pot, combine the apple cider, dried apples, applesauce, lemon juice, raisins, brown sugar, coriander seeds, vanilla, cinnamon, cloves, and nutmeg. Bring to a boil over high heat. Lower the heat and simmer for at least 1 hour to reduce the liquid.
2. Trappers' Fruit will be ready to eat whenever you're ready to eat it. At The Fort we like to cook it, covered, for several hours, stirring frequently to prevent burning. Just before serving, stir in the toasted hazelnuts and add the rum.

CHAPTER 7

FRONTIER DRINK

LIFE IN THE EARLY FORTS OF THE WEST WAS NOT AS primitive as one might think. Although beaver tail, raw buffalo liver, and dog stew often graced the table, the bourgeois, or boss man, of the fort ate off English porcelain and wiped his mouth with damask napkins. Most forts had wine cellars that featured French and Spanish wines: Bordeaux wines from France, Tenerife wine from the Canary Islands, ports, sherries, clarets, and fine Madeira vied with an occasional bottle of French Champagne as favorites.

Wines were usually sold by the hogshead or pipe (a pipe was two hogsheads or 105 gallons). Wine was decanted from these barrels into hand-blown glass bottles, supplied empty to the buyer. In fact, bottles were so rare on the frontier that a 25-cent bottle of whiskey bought in St. Louis and drained along the Santa Fe Trail, brought in 50 cents in New Mexico.

Many Americans, eager for the dollar, operated stills in Taos, New Mexico, which was then under Mexican rule. The liquor, fermented from wheat, was called Taos lightning. No one knows how much alcohol came north through trading, but with five distilleries in Taos running full time by 1846, the amount must have been considerable.

Tremendous profits were to be made from the sale of alcohol, sometimes amounting to 10,000 percent. This was such a lucrative business, much of the alcohol was cut with large amounts of water to help the bottom line. To mask this dilution, early traders added gunpowder, red pepper and tobacco tea to the liquor.

Traders Whiskey

Even when quality whiskey made it west in the 1860s, the Indians resisted it, preferring the flavor of the liquor they had become used to. Unscrupulous traders at Fort Laramie doctored their traders whiskey with laudanum (tincture of opium) in order to prevent violence after nights of heavy drinking. Some of the Indians who drank this overdosed and died. When whiskey was traded at Indian camps, the chief sampled the contents of each barrel to assure fellow tribesmen that the spirit was worth the furs being traded.

If you try this, use old-fashioned black gunpowder made of saltpeter, sulfur, and charcoal. Modern nitrated, high-speed powders are poisonous.

serves 16; makes 16 shots

3 or 4 small, whole hot red peppers, fresh or dried

Cut plug tobacco or tobacco from 2 cigarettes

1 quart corn whiskey or bourbon

A thumb pinch old-fashioned black gunpowder (not modern gunpowder)

1. In a small pot, heat the peppers in ½ cup water over high heat for 10 minutes to make a tea. Strain. Return the tea to the pot and cook over medium-high heat until it reduces to ¼ cup.

2. In another small pot, boil the tobacco in ½ cup water for 10 minutes. Strain. Return the liquid to the pot and cook over medium-high heat until it reduces to ¼ cup.

3. Add both of the reduced liquids to the whiskey and put a pinch of gunpowder in the bottle. The pinch of black gunpowder gives a special smooth taste.

Hailstorm

The hailstorm is a primitive mint julep that was traditionally served on the 4th of July at southern Colorado's Bent's Fort. The fort was active in the 1830s and was the hub of a vast network of Indian trading and the freighting business from Missouri to Santa Fe. Ice was cut from the nearby Arkansas River and stored in an ice house and wild mint grew nearby. Celebrants added some sort of whiskey to these to mark the birth of the United States. The whiskey could have been Taos Lightning, distilled from wheat, or it could have been quentogue juisque, *which was Kentucky whiskey.*

Hailstorms make marvelous party drinks because they can be made ahead: put the mint, sugar and whiskey in glass jars with lids. When it's time to serve them, fill the jars with cracked ice and hand a jar to your guest, who can shake it lustily until the mint leaves are bruised and release their wonderful flavor. Granulated sugar is nearly as good as powdered sugar for this purpose. One hailstorm is a quite sufficient dosage.

serves 1

3 ounces bourbon or Scotch whiskey
1 tablespoon powdered sugar
1 sprig fresh mint
Crushed ice to fill the jar

Combine the whiskey, sugar, and mint in a ½-liter or wide-mouth canning jar with lid. Add crushed ice. Shake until the mint leaves are bruised.

Haymaker's Switchel

Rum and applejack were extremely popular in early America and when mixed together, make a fine drink called a "switchel." Some haymaker's switchels are non-alcoholic, made with molasses, vinegar, and powdered ginger and are surprisinlgy refreshing with a pleasant, sweet-and-sour spiciness. Temperance groups believed applejack was a major public menace and literally cut down hundreds of apple orchards across the country to prevent anyone from making apple brandy.

serves 16 to 18

2 cups apple cider vinegar
1 cup brown sugar
½ cup light molasses, or more to taste
1 teaspoon powdered ginger, optional

Combine 3 quarts of cold water with the vinegar, brown sugar, molasses, and ginger, if using. Stir to dissolve the sugar. Taste and add more molasses, if desired. Serve over ice.

★ CHAMPAGNE IN WYOMING

Champagne was not unknown in the West. The earliest record of it being drunk at Wyoming's Fort William, later known as Fort Laramie, was in 1832 when a young man carefully carried a bottle with him and popped its cork at the fort. Alas, this farsighted person's name is lost to the ages. In later years, the fort boasted a first-rate wine cellar and a wide range of fine liquors. These were sometimes enjoyed with caviar.

Atole

References to drinking atole *are common, and usually identify it as a basic Mexican-Indian gruel.* Harina de atole, *which is toasted and finely ground blue cornmeal, is often found in the Mexican food section of supermarkets, next to the packages of dried chiles and cinnamon sticks. If you can't find it, substitute masa harina, the ground hominy meal used to make tortillas and tamales. Try this with a little red chile, chopped and sprinkled over the top, or a dollop of Basic Red Chile Puree on page 48.*

serves 4 to 6

3 to 4 cups beef broth or water
1 cup atole flour or masa harina
½ teaspoon kosher salt

In a saucepan, cook the broth and flour over low heat, stirring constantly for 6 to 8 minutes or until the mixture thickens and is smooth. It will have the texture of thick hot chocolate. If it seems too thick, stir in a little more broth or water. Season to taste with salt and serve.

Pinole

The terms used to describe Mexican and Indian foods vary wildly and a good historian is suspicious of them all, knowing that local terminology is rarely universal. For example, atole (see page 101) may be called pinole, and vice versa. The difference usually is that pinole is sweetened for a healthful, nourishing and delicious drink.

serves 4 to 6

1 cup finely ground cornmeal or atole flour
¼ cup sugar
½ teaspoon ground cinnamon
3 to 4 cups milk
½ teaspoon kosher salt

1. Preheat the oven to 450°F.
2. Spread the cornmeal evenly in a rimmed baking sheet and roast it in the oven for 4 to 6 minutes until golden brown. Take care it does not burn. (If using atole flour, skip this step. It is already toasted.) Stir with a spoon two or three times during roasting. Remove the baking sheet from the oven and let the cornmeal cool on the sheet.
3. Transfer the cornmeal to a large saucepan. Add the sugar and cinnamon to the cornmeal and then ½ cup of cold water to moisten
4. Stir in the milk and cook over low heat, stirring constantly, for about 15 minutes. Be careful the cornmeal does not burn on the bottom of the saucepan. The pinole is done when it's the texture of thick hot chocolate. If too thick, thin with additional milk or water.

Mexican Hot Chocolate

Early visitors to the Southwest found Mexicans enjoying a thick hot chocolate with a consistency and flavor quite different from the hot chocolate they knew from back East.

The chocolate used to make Mexican hot chocolate contains sugar, cinnamon, and a bit of vanilla as well as dark chocolate. It is commonly formed into rounded tablets that are dissolved in hot milk. These tablets are often found in the Mexican foods section of supermarkets.

serves 4 to 6

4 cups milk or water
6 ounces Mexican chocolate, roughly chopped

1. In a large saucepan, bring the milk to a simmer over medium-high heat. Add the chocolate and immediately reduce the heat to low.
2. With a wire whisk or hand-held electric mixer, whip the chocolate over low heat until the pieces melt and a layer of foam forms on top.
3. Serve the chocolate in cups and spoon the foam onto the top.

Tea and Coffee in the West

DURING THE MID 1800S, BOTH COFFEE AND TEA WERE thought to have medicinal value and were advised for prevention of headaches, gout and "gravel." In the early American West, sassafras tea was a regularly used tonic and was sought after by mountain man and pioneers alike. Today, you can still finds sassafras tea at fancy groceries and in health food stores.

Coffee beans were sold green until shortly after the Civil War and roasting and grinding were up to the buyer. Over time, the Arbuckle brothers of Pittsburgh, Pennsylvania, developed a method for coating roasted coffee beans with a mixture of egg white and sugar. This treatment prevented oxidation and held in the roasted flavor — and meant the beans could be shipped anywhere, already roasted.

Arbuckle's became famous in the West and the name was synonymous with coffee. Cowboys were known to speculate gloomily that coffee might not be available after the Arbuckles died! At one time, each brown paper bag of Arbuckle's coffee had a stick of peppermint candy, tucked in with the beans as a premium. Cowboys were more than happy to grind the coffee beans in order to get the candy — and sometimes fisticuffs ensued! In addition to the peppermint, Arbuckle's offered another premium. The labels from the packages could be redeemed for men's razors, alarm clocks, and the like.

Old-Style Campfire Coffee

Campfire coffee often was made in a pot and so the trappers and traders devised a way to keep the grounds out of the brew. The egg was added to clarify the brew, a trick cooks have long known about. The coffee is absolutely superb.

serves 4 to 6

1 cup ground coffee beans
1 large egg

1. In a large pot, bring 1 quart of cold water to a boil over high heat and let it boil for 2 to 3 minutes.
2. Meanwhile, lay a piece of cheesecloth on a work surface and put the coffee and the egg, still in its shell, in the middle and tie the cheesecloth into a sack. Break the egg in the sack by rapping it against the countertop and massage the bag to mix the egg with the coffee. Drop the sack into the boiling water and cook for 4 minutes.
3. Add ½ cup cold water to the pot to settle any grounds. Remove the sack, if you want to, and pour the coffee into mugs.

CHAPTER 8

Mormon Foods

FROM ITS FOUNDING IN 1830, MORMONISM HAS BEEN A missionary religion, a powerful force that brought thousands of enthusiastic converts to the Promised Land in Utah. The zeal of these Saints, as they were known because they were members of the Church of Jesus Christ of Latter-Day Saints, grew to such a high pitch by the middle of the 19th century that they offered to walk across the country — even from England, Ireland, Scotland, Denmark, Sweden and Switzerland.

Thousands of impoverished people heeded the call but by 1855, both money and food were scarce and only one in 20 Saints could be transported to Utah. Brigham Young devised another plan to help immigrants reach their destination. They could reach Iowa City by rail and from there walk the rest of the way, hauling their belongings in a handcart. The journey was treacherous, taking the travelers across the plains and over mountains.

One traveler wrote, "Hitherto, although a ration of a pound of flour had been served out daily to each person, it was found insufficient to satisfy the cravings of hunger. Shortly after leaving Fort Laramie it became necessary to shorten our rations that they might hold out and that the company not be reduced to starvation. First the pound of flour was reduced to three-fourths, then to a half pound, and afterward to still less per day. However we pushed ahead."

As winter set in, starvation was severe. One group was reduced to eating rawhide, which at first made them sick. Jones, a professional cook, devised a plan to make rawhide palatable. "Scorch and scrape the hair off; this has a tendency to kill and purify the bad taste that scalding gave it," he wrote. "After scraping, boil one hour throwing the water away that had extracted all the glue then wash and let it get cold and then eat with a little sugar sprinkled on it."

Fruit Soup

Ten companies of Saints, as Mormons were called, traveled the handcart route between 1856 and 1860. The dedication and heroism of these travelers has rarely been equaled. In later years, Mormon cooking recognized its culinary heritage as coming from New England, the British Isles, Scandinavia and Switzerland. Old recipes were adapted for the foods found in the West. One such dish is a fruit soup, based on those that originated in Scandinavia. Serve this soup at the beginning of a meal or at the end, as dessert.

serves 12 to 14; makes about 3 quarts

½ pound raisins
½ pound prunes
½ pound currants
¼ pound red raspberries
3 tart apples, such as Granny Smith, cored and chopped
Juice of ½ small lemon
1 cinnamon stick
3 to 4 tablespoons sugar, optional
1½ teaspoons cornstarch or white sago, see Note

1. In a large pot, mix the raisins, prunes, currants, raspberries, apples, lemon juice, and cinnamon stick with 2 quarts (8 cups) of water. Bring to a boil over medium-high heat, reduce the heat to low, cover, and simmer for about 45 minutes, or until the fruit is softened.

2. Taste the soup and add sugar, if needed. Remove the cinnamon stick.
3. Mix the cornstarch with a little water to make a slurry and add to the soup. If using sago, see Note. Cook the soup for 3 to 4 minutes longer, stirring, to thicken. Serve the soup hot or chilled. The soup will keep for up to 3 days in the refrigerator.

Note: Sago is a starch from the stem of a West Indian palm and is most easily found in stores selling Middle Eastern foods, where it might be labeled pearlized tapioca. Follow the package instructions for how to use it. It has long had a place in American cooking; George Washington evidently had a sago palm at Mt. Vernon.

Sago Rhubarb Pudding

Rhubarb was one of the mainstays of the Mormon diet. Settlers brought rhubarb roots wrapped in dampened cloths or packed in cans of dirt to plant in their new homes. The vitamin-filled root provides protection from scurvy and is overall healthful in any diet. Rhubarb pudding made with sago is an authentic and delicious Mormon dish. It resembles a topping or sauce to modern folks; try it spooned over ice cream or pound cake.

serves 12 to 14; makes about 3 quarts

1 cup small white sago (pearlized tapioca)
4 cups tepid water
Pinch of salt
1 pound fresh or frozen rhubarb, cut into bite-sized pieces (½ to 1 inch wide)
⅔ cup sugar

1. Rinse the sago in cool, running water 3 times.
2. In a mixing bowl, mix the sago with the tepid water and salt. Set aside to soak for 1 hour.
3. Transfer the water and sago to a saucepan and bring to a boil over medium-high heat. Reduce the heat to low, cover the pan, and simmer for about 2 hours, stirring occasionally, until the water turns slightly clear and to prevent sticking. Add 4 to 5 more cups of water as needed to thin the liquid and allow the sago to swell and soften.
4. Add the rhubarb and sugar and cook for about 10 minutes, or until the rhubarb softens. (Frozen rhubarb may cook in 4 to 5 minutes.) Remove from the heat and serve warm or chilled.

In Search of Sweet

Early Mormon women used pumpkins, which grew profusely in their new home, to make a sweet syrup to replace sugar. These ingenious home cooks cut a hole in the top of the squash, cleaned out the insides and then left the pumpkins outdoors during cold nights for several days. The juices gathered in the pumpkins and the Mormon cooks could then boil them into a sugary syrup.

Records exist of the Mormons in Utah finding "manna" on the leaves of certain trees. The substance was sweet and came to be known as Mormon sugar. The Spanish in California had earlier discovered the same thing. Only recently has the crystallized substance been identified as the droppings of aphids.

Sugar was a great delicacy and although pumpkin syrup and Mormon sugar were sweet substitutes, honey was more often the sweetener of choice when cane sugar was not available. It should be noted, however, that honey bees were not native to the Americas. The honey bee was imported from England with early settlers and immediately found a lot of flora with ample pollen and started producing honey.

The Indians were not familiar with honey bees and in fact, they usually knew when it was time to move further west, ahead of the white man, when honey bees were spotted in their territory.

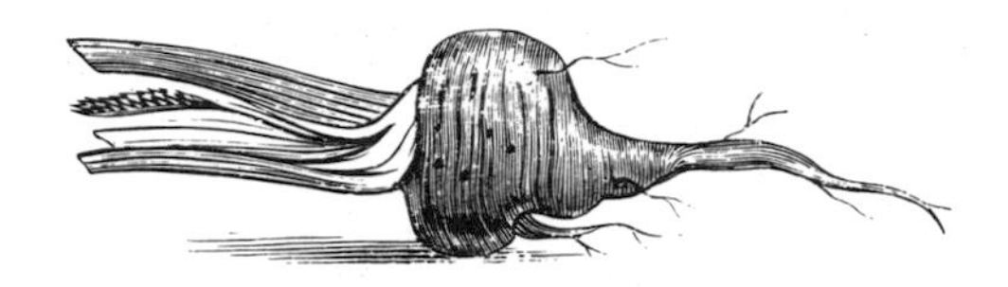

Red Flannel Hash

Mormons from northern New England brought an old Vermont recipe with them, one that reputedly was popular with Ethan Allen and his Green Mountain Boys during the American Revolution. Called red flannel hash because of the beets, it's a good breakfast or supper dish, especially with fried or poached eggs on top. When you have some leftover baked potatoes and roasted beets, try this.

serves 4 to 6

3 medium beets, roasted, peeled and chopped
1 large potato, baked, peeled and chopped
1 pound ground chuck beef
Salt and freshly ground black pepper
6 tablespoons unsalted butter
1 medium onion, chopped
2 tablespoons heavy cream

1. In a mixing bowl, mix together the beets, potato and beef. Season lightly with salt and pepper.

2. In a large skillet, heat 4 tablespoons of butter over medium-high heat. Add the onion and cook until the onion is translucent, 3 to 4 minutes. Stir in the meat mixture and cook, stirring, for 8 to 10 minutes or until the meat is cooked through.

3. Transfer the hash to a shallow 10-by-12-inch broiler-safe pan, or one that is similar in size, and spread out in an even layer. Alternatively, spread the hash in a skillet.

4. In a small saucepan, melt the remaining 2 tablespoons of butter in the cream. When melted, pour this over the hash.

5. Broil the hash for 3 to 4 minutes or until a crispy crust forms. Alternatively, fry the hash in a skillet for 3 to 4 minutes, or until crispy on the bottom. Serve hot.

Colcannon

This is another typical dish found in Mormon homes when the Saints first settled near modern-day Salt Lake City. Its roots are in Ireland, where it usually was made with cabbage and potatoes. Spinach is a good stand-in for cabbage in this comforting dish.

serves 6

4 medium potatoes, peeled, boiled and mashed
1 cup cooked, chopped spinach, drained
2 tablespoons unsalted butter, cut into pats
Salt and freshly ground black pepper

1. Preheat the oven to 375°F. Lightly oil an 8-by-12-by-2-inch baking dish, or one of similar size. A 2-quart oval or round baking dish works well, too.
2. In a mixing bowl, mix together the potatoes and spinach. Lay the butter pats over the top of the vegetables and season with salt and pepper. Bake for about 10 minutes or until heated all the way through.

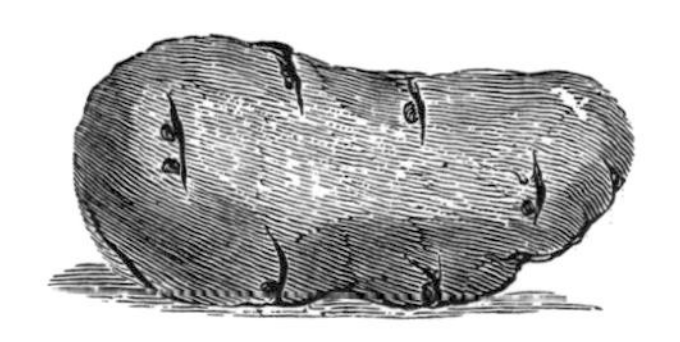

Potato Balls

These surprisingly light, fried potato balls are one of my favorite Mormon recipes. I found the recipe in a 1961 cookbook by Kate B. Carter called The Pioneer Cookbook *and published by Utah Printing Company based — where else? — in Salt Lake City.*

serves 4 to 6; makes 16 potato balls

4 medium potatoes, mashed
1 egg yolk
Salt and freshly ground black pepper
1 large egg, lightly beaten
¾ cup cracker crumbs, such as saltines and Ritz
Vegetable oil, for frying

1. In a mixing bowl, mix together the mashed potatoes with the egg yolk and season with salt and pepper. Using your hands, form the mixture into golf ball-sized balls.
2. Put the beaten egg in a shallow bowl and the cracker crumbs in another. Dip the potato balls first in the egg and then in the crackers, turning to coat. Set aside on dish.
3. In a large, deep heavy pot, heat 3 inches of oil to 325°F. until it's hot and shimmering.
4. Using a long-handled slotted spoon, submerge 2 to 4 of the coated potato balls in the hot oil and fry until crispy and cooked through, about 2 minutes. Lift the potato balls from the oil and drain on paper towels. Let the oil regain its temperature before frying more potato balls. Season with salt and serve immediately.

CHAPTER 9

CHRISTMAS SPECIALS

CHRISTMAS TIME IN OLD SANTA FE IS A DELIGHTFUL experience. The cool crisp winter air is perfumed with smoke from piñon and native cedar fires. On Christmas Eve, many Santa Feans travel south about 40 miles to a wonderful Indian pueblo called San Felipe for a very special celebration. My most vivid Christmas Eve memory is from 1948. I arrived at the pueblo at about eleven that night to find the pueblo's little church lit with oil lamps and candles. Indians in costume danced up to the altar in a serious prayer ceremony, which lasted about 20 minutes and ended with the priest leading the midnight mass in Latin. It was a truly moving experience.

Biscochitos

As part of our Santa Fe Christmas Tradition, we went to Joe Esquibel's house on east De Vargas Street. There we ate biscochitos, wonderful anise-cinnamon flavored cookies that usually were served with alongside steaming hot coffee brewed from clear, Indian pueblo well water.

makes 4 to 5 dozen (2 to 3 inch) cookies

3 large eggs
1 cup (8 ounces) lard or solid vegetable shortening
2 cups sifted all-purpose flour + more as needed
1 cup sugar
1 tablespoon anise seeds
1 large egg white
1 teaspoon rum or bourbon
Ground cinnamon or colored decorating sugars

1. In a medium mixing bowl, whisk the 3 eggs until well combined.
2. In the bowl of an electric mixer, cut the lard into the flour with a pastry blender or 2 forks until the mixture starts to be crumbly. Add the sugar and mix well. Alternatively, use a hand-held electric mixer to mix the ingredients together.
3. Add the beaten eggs and anise seeds and gradually add more flour to make a firm dough, if needed. Divide the dough into 2 to 3 portions, wrap each in plastic wrap, and refrigerate for at least 30 minutes or until firm.

4. Preheat the oven to 350°F. Position a rack in the center of the oven. Line 2 baking sheets with parchment or silicon baking mats.
5. Roll out the chilled dough, a portion at a time, on a lightly floured surface to a thickness of 1/4 inch.
6. Dip a 2- to 3-inch cookie cutter into a little flour and cut out your favorite cookie shapes. Arrange the cookies on the baking sheets, leaving about an inch between each one.
7. In a small bowl, beat the egg white with the rum until frothy. Brush the tops of the cookies lightly with the egg wash and sprinkle with cinnamon.
8. Bake the biscochitos, 1 baking sheet at a time, for 3 to 5 minutes, or until barely brown. Transfer them to a rack to cool.

★ GENTLY GLOWING CHRISTMAS TRADITIONS

A lovely Christmas tradition in New Mexico is the use of farolitos and luminarias. Farolitos, or little lanterns, are easily made by filling small, brown paper bags with sand or kitty litter, folding down the tops of the sacks about 2 inches to stabilize them, and then inserting a long-burning candle in each bag. When placed along walks, around porches, or on the roof lines of a building, the farolitos shine a cheery yellowish light in the chilly night.

Many people mistakenly call farolitos "luminarias." In fact, luminarias are stacks of pitch pine, piled in a crossed pattern, and then lit to make a bright bonfire. These were being ignited by the Moors in Spain long before the Christian religion arrived there and being a very long-lived Spanish tradition, happily have been adopted as part of the Christmas traditions of the Southwest.

Holiday Bird Stuffing

The Spanish pine, or piñon, produces fine small nuts, which are sold commercially everywhere. If you are lucky enough to live where the pine trees grow, you can gather your own. Some New Mexicans wait until the first snow falls to forage for piñon nuts (also referred to as seeds). They follow ground squirrel or chipmunk trails to underground burrows where the animals have stashed quantities of the seeds for the coming winter. Nice people leave some for squirrels! Piñon nuts are best hulled after they are roasted by cracking the shells in your teeth. As delicious as they are on their own, they also add outstanding flavor to the stuffing for a holiday bird.

serves 8 to 10;
makes enough stuffing for a 12- to 15-pound turkey

2 medium russet (Idaho) potatoes, peeled and diced
6 tablespoons unsalted butter
2 cups chopped fresh apples (about 2 apples)
1 cup chopped onion
1 teaspoon dried thyme
1 teaspoon rubbed sage
½ teaspoon kosher salt, or more to taste
¼ teaspoon freshly ground black pepper, or more to taste
1 large egg
½ cup diced mild green chiles (4-ounce can)
½ cup roasted, shelled piñon nuts
4 cups dry bread cubes (6 to 8 bread slices)

1. Put the potatoes in a large saucepan and add enough water to cover by an inch or two. Lightly salt the water and then bring it to a boil over high heat. Reduce the heat to medium-low and cook until tender, about 20 minutes. Drain the potatoes; cover and steam for a few minutes. Rice or mash the potatoes and set aside.
2. In a large skillet, melt the butter over medium heat. Add the apples, onion, thyme, and sage and cook, stirring, for 5 to 7 minutes or until the onion is translucent. Fold this mixture into the potatoes. Season with salt and pepper and set aside to cool until just warm.
3. Transfer the potatoes to a large bowl and mix in the egg. Stir in the green chiles and piñon nuts and then gently fold in the bread cubes. If the mixture seems dry, moisten it with a little chicken broth or water. Refrigerate until ready to cook.
4. Preheat the oven to 350°F.
5. Loosely stuff into the buttered neck and body cavities of a 12 to 15-pound turkey and roast according to a recipe for stuffed turkey, or bake the stuffing in a buttered baking dish for about 45 minutes or until the top is golden brown and crusty and the stuffing is heated throughout.

Cherry Bounce

Cherry Bounce figures into one of my favorite memories from western Christmas celebrations. It is related to the early American "shrubs" — combinations of fruit and brandy or rum. When made properly, the bounce resembles a delightfully syrupy liqueur that will let you sip yourself to paradise. This is an early American recipe that will make history come to life for your holiday guests.

serves 16 to 20

5 pints dark cherries
1 quart dark rum or cognac
1 pound brown sugar

1. Grind the cherries through a meat grinder, seeds and all. Transfer the ground cherries to a bottle holding the rum or cognac. Cap or cork the bottle and set aside at room temperature for at least 1 week, or a little longer if you can stand to wait.
2. Strain the liquor through cheesecloth into a bowl. Stir the sugar into it and when the sugar dissolves, pour the bounce into a jug. Cork the jug and set aside for 2 weeks before serving.

Yard of Flannel

While this holiday libation may be an acquired taste, once you acquire it you will be in love. It marries the hoppy taste of beer with the warmth of rum-based eggnog and, as they say, will "warm the cockles of your heart" on a snowy evening. When I researched the cocktail, I discovered this passage: "A fine colonial winter specialty in taverns, this hot ale drink takes its name from its lovely soft texture. The Yard of Flannel is a wonderful holiday drink that used to be a favorite among coachmen, outriders, and wagoneers. Coming out of the tavern, bartenders would hand up a yard-long glass of this to freezing coach drivers perched high above. The recipe sounds far more complicated than it is, and is worth the effort in the resulting warmth of body and soul."

serves 4

1 quart good ale
4 large eggs
4 tablespoons sugar
1 teaspoon powdered ginger
4 ounces Jamaica dark rum
Grated nutmeg, for sprinkling

Heat the ale in a saucepan. In a blender, beat the eggs with the sugar. Add the ginger and then the rum and blend well. When the ale is almost boiling, slowly combine the two mixtures, alternately pouring the hot ale, a little at a time, into the egg mixture and blending well, to prevent curdling. Pour back and forth between the saucepan and the blender until the drink is silky or as soft as flannel. Serve in a large glass sprinkled with nutmeg.

Hangman's Eggnog

During the 1600s, British seamen drank punch generally made from five ingredients: tea, water, arrack, sugar, and lemon. Arrack is an Asian liquor made from palm sugar that was replaced by rum in the 1700s. To this day, rum punch is a favorite holiday libation. In the old days, Christmas drinks were higher in protein than alcohol and two American favorites were Hangman's Eggnog and Yard of Flannel.

Eggnog came from the term "noggin," which was the name for solid birch wood drinking containers. Noggins were used at table, while tankards, made from staves and hoops, were more common at the fireside. Present-day eggnog began as a "dry sack posset," dry sack being the English name for dry Spanish wine and sherry. The result of heating dry wine with eggs was called eggnog. This recipe is for a rich, delicious drink that is perfect for a Christmas party, although in the Old West it also was traditionally drunk after a hanging as well.

serves 8 to 10

3½ cups whole milk

6 large egg yolks

½ cup sugar

1½ tablespoons cornstarch

⅔ cup bourbon

⅓ cup Jamaican rum

1 cup (½ pint) heavy cream

Freshly grated nutmeg

1. In the top of a double boiler, mix 3 cups of the milk with the eggs and sugar and whisk until smooth. (Do not cook this mixture yet.)

2. In a small bowl, combine the remaining ½ cup of milk with the cornstarch to make a thin paste.

3. Set the top of the double boiler over enough hot water to almost touch the bottom of the pot and gently cook the custard over medium-low heat, stirring constantly, until it is nearly simmering. At this point, stir in the cornstarch mixture and stir for 10 to 15 minutes until the custard thickens enough to coat the back of a spoon or spatula.

4. Remove the eggnog from the heat and stir in the bourbon and rum. Transfer to a serving bowl and chill for at least 2 hours or until very cold.

5. Just before serving, whip the cream to soft peaks. Fold the whipped cream into the eggnog and ladle the nog into cups. Sprinkle the top with freshly grated nutmeg.

Where to Find It

Achiote Paste
La Perla Spice Company
555 N. Fairview St.
Santa Ana, California 92703
(800) 335-6292 www.shop.delmayab.com

Aluminum Foil Smoking Bags
Hot Diggity Cajun
(888) 831-9674 www.hotdiggitycajun.com

My Secret Pantry
5135 E. Ingram St.
Mesa, Arizona 85205
(866) 440-2811 www.mysecretpantry.com

Buffalo Meat and Tongue
Altavista Bison
80 Hillside Road
Rutland, Massachusetts 01543
(508) 886-4365 www.altavistabison.com

Cushman Bison Farms
10225 W. 34 Road
Harrietta, Michigan 49638
www.CushmanBisonFarms.com

Great Range Bison
9757 Alton Way
Denver, Colorado 80640
(800) 327-2706 (303) 287-7100
(303) 287-7272 (fax)
www.greatrangebison.com

Liechty Buffalo Ranch
P.O. Box 36
Leo, Indiana 46765 (260) 627-0124
www.liechtybuffaloranch.com

Chiles and Ristras
The Chile Shop
109 East Water St.
Santa Fe, New Mexico 87501
(505) 983-6080 (505) 984-0737
www.thechileshop.com

Curry Bush Leaves
My Spice Sage
5774 Mosholu Avenue
Bronx, New York 10471
(877) 890-5244 www.myspicesage.com

Dried Damiana
EGarden Seed
(707) 733-3710
www.egardenseed.com

Quality Bulk Herbs
Deerfield Beach, Florida 33441
(619) 940-4516
www.QualityBulkHerbs.com

Grits
Agrirama
Georgia's Museum of Agriculture
& Historic Village
1392 Whiddon Mill Road
Tifton, Georgia 31793
(800) 776-1875 (229) 386-7289
www.agrirama.com

Local Harvest
P.O. Box 1292
Santa Cruz, California 95061
(831) 515-5602 www.localharvest.org

Southern Grace Farms
Rt.1 Box 28A
Enigma, Georgia 31749 (229) 533-8585
www.southerngracefarms.net

Heirloom Beans
Adobe Milling Company
P.O. Box 596
Dove Creek, Colorado 81324
(800) 542-3623 www.anasazibeans.com

Purcell Mountains Farms
Moyie Springs, Idaho 83845
(208) 267-0627
www.purcellmountainfarms.com

Rancho Gordo
1924 Yajome
Napa, California 94559 (707) 259-1935
www.RanchoGordo.com

Huckleberry Preserves
Eva Gates Homemade Preserves
PO Box 696
Bigfork, Montana 59911 (800) 682-4283
www.evagates.com

Huckleberry Morning
P.O. Box 190387
Hungry Horse, Montana 59919
(406) 387-4227
www.huckleberrymorning.com

The Huckleberry Patch Gift Shop
8868 US Highway 2 East
Hungry Horse, Montana 59919
(800) 527-7340
www.huckleberrypatch.com

Indian Garden Seeds
Museum of the Fur Trade
Highway 20
Chadron, Nebraska 69337 (308) 432-3843
www.furtrade.org
The museum saves enough of the precious seeds to replant, and any surplus is offered for sale to museum patrons.

Lamb Spareribs
Lava Lake Land & Livestock, L.L.C.
P.O. Box 2249
Hailey, Idaho 83333 (888) 528-5253
www.lavalakelamb.com/

U.S. Wellness Meats
P.O. Box 9
Monticello, Missouri 63457
(877) 383-0051 www.grasslandbeef.com

Mexican Jalapeños in Jars
Mex Grocer
(877) 463-9476
www.mexgrocer.com

Prickly Pear Syrup
Cheri's Desert Harvest
1840 E. Winsett
Tucson, Arizona 85719
(800) 743-1141 (520) 623-4141
www.cherisdesertharvest.com

Quail, Quail Eggs, and Other Game Birds
Manchester Farms, Inc.
P.O. Box 97
Dalzell, South Carolina 29040
(800) 845-0421 (803) 469-8637 (fax)
www.manchesterfarms.com

Lake Cumberland Game Bird Farm
7768 East Highway 90
Monticello Wayne, Kentucky 42633
(765) 381-3642 (606) 348-6370 (fax)
www.lakecumberlandgamebirds.com

Quinoa and San Luis Potatoes
White Mountain Farms
8890 Lane 4 North
Mosca, Colorado 81146
(800) 364-3019
(719) 378-2436
www.whitemountainfarms.com

Spanish Spices, Saffron, Sausages, and Cookware
The Spanish Table
109 North Guadalupe St.
Santa Fe, New Mexico 87501
(505) 986-0243
www.spanishtable.com

Index

a

ale, 123
apple brandy, 100
apple pie without apples, 90-91
applejack, 100
apples, 94-95, 108, 120-121
applesauce, 94-95
Arnold, Sam, 6-9, 52
atole, 101

b

bacon, 16-17, 38-39, 66-67, 78-79
baked Indian pudding, 72-73
baked stuffed pumpkin, 68-69
bannock bread, 83
basic red chile puree, 48
beans
  black, 66
  navy, 66
  pinto, 56, 66
beefsteak and oysters, 27
beer, 123
before metal kettles, 67
berries, 17, 44, 70, 87, 92
bison, 24-26
biscochitos, 118-119
black-eyed peas, 16
blue Indian cornmeal tamale pie, 62-63
blueberries, 44
bourbon, 98, 99, 124-125
buffalo, 17, 20, 22, 24-26, 37, 68-70, 97
  on the prairie, 26
buffalo tongue, 24

c

cabbage, 30, 114
capers, 24-25, 30
capirotada, 93
carne asada, 49
cedar wood cooking planks, 44
cheese
  goat, 56
  monterey jack, 32, 56, 62, 64
cherries, 22-23, 70, 71, 122
cherry bounce, 122
chess pie, 86, 88
chicken, 30-31, 32-33, 52, 64, 68-69, 72
chiles, 32-33, 42, 46-57, 62-67, 101, 120-121
  about, 50-51,
  how to work with, 55
chocolate, 103
Christmas, 116-125
cider-cooked trappers' fruit, 94-95
coconut, 16
coffee, 104, 105, 118
coffee beans, 104, 105

colcannon, 114
corn, 20-21, 32-33, 52-53, 56-57, 59-64, 68-69, 75, 82,
about, 75
dried, 20
corn and bean chile soup, 56-57
corn tortillas, 32-33
cornbread, 75, 78-79
cornmeal, 43, 62-65, 70-73, 75, 78-79, 82, 102
croutons, 53, 56-57
currants, 83, 108

d

deer, 20, 22, 37
dried cranberries, 72, 83

e

edible cooking vessel , 67
eggnog, 123-125
enchiladas, 32

f

farolitos, 119
fish, 36-39, 44-45
flour tortillas, 64
Fort Laramie, 14, 29, 30, 72, 76, 98, 100, 107
Fort Laramie chicken salad, 30-31
Fort-style buffalo tongue with caper sauce, 24-25
fried salt pork gravy, 15
frijoles, 66-67
fruit soup, 108-109
fry bread, 80-81
Frying Pans West, 6-0, 20

g

Grant, Ulysses S., 24, 42
gravy, 15, 16
green chile steak bowl, 54
gunpowder, 97-98

h

hailstorm, 99
hangman's eggnog, 124-125
hangtown fry, 40-41
haymaker's switchel, 100
hazelnuts, 94-95
holiday bird stuffing, 120-121
hominy, 64-65, 101
honey, 44-45, 80-81, 90-91
hoppin' john, 15, 16-17
horseradish, 24-25
huckleberry, 44-45

i

in search of sweet, 111
Indian foods, 58-73
Indian fry bread, 80-81
Indian pemmican, 22
Indian Pudding, 72-73

j

Jamaican pickapeppa sauce, 19
jerky, 18-23

l

Lakota Indian fry bread, 80-81
lanterns, 119
Lincoln, Abraham, 43
Lind, Jenny 24
Linghams chili sauce, 19

m

Magoffin, Susan Shelby, 56
marrow, 17
masa harina, 101
Mexican hot chocolate, 103
Mexican oregano, 48-49, 54, 56, 62
minted trout, 38-39
Mohawk Indian corn, 60-61
moose, 6-7
Mormons, 106-115
mountain men, 25
music, 29

n

Native Americans 64, 67, 75, 83, 94
new year's day, 16

o

old-fashioned potato bread, 76-77
old-style campfire coffee, 105
oregano, Mexican, 48-49, 54, 56, 62
oysters, 27-28, 34, 40-43

p

PBS Television, 9
pemmican, 22-23, 70, 94
peppers
  chiles, 32-33, 42, 46-57, 62-67, 101, 120-121
  hot red, 98
  jalapeño, 50
pickled oysters, 42
pie, 62-63, 86-91
pies and tarts, 87
piki bread, 79
pinole, 102
planked salmon, 44-45
pork, 64-65
  shoulder, 64
  posole, 64-65
  posole with pork and red chile, 64-65
potato balls, 115
potato bread, 76-77
potatoes, 76, 112-113, 115
prairie butter, 17
prairie potatoes, 20
prairie turnips, 18
prunes, 108
pumpkin, 68-69, 111
  sugar, 68

r

raspberries, 108
red flannel hash, 112-113
rhubarb, 110
rice, 16-17, 52
Rocky Mountain oysters, 34-35
rum, 94-95, 100, 118-119, 122, 123, 124-125

s

sago, 108-110
sago rhubarb pudding, 110
salmon, 44-45
salt pork, 12-16, 66-67
salt pork gravy, 15
skillet cornbread, 78-79
split peas, 12
squash, 59, 68, 111
steak, 27-28, 49, 54
  beef tenderloin, 54
  beefsteak, 27
  loin strip, 54
  skirt, 49
stewed hen in red chile, 52-53
stuffing, 120-121
suet, 22-23
sunflower seeds, 68-69
Swiss enchilada, 32-33

t

tamales, 62, 101
tea, 97, 98, 104, 124
  sassafras, 104
Tesoro Cultural Center, 8
the Fort restaurant, 6-9, 25, 30, 33, 34
tobacco, 97, 98
tongue, 24-25
tortillas, 54, 82
  flour tortillas, 64
  corn tortillas, 32-33
transparent pie, 88-89
trout, 37-39

v

voyageurs' pea soup, 12-13

w

walnuts
  black, 60-61
  english, 60
washtunkala, 20-21
was-nah
  Indian version, 70
  modern version, 71
what I know about chiles, 50-51
where to find it, 126-127
whiskey, 97, 98, 99
white eyes wo-japi, 92
wines, 97

y

yard of flannel, 123, 124